Challenging
E-Learning in
the University

A literacies perspective

Robin Goodfellow and
Mary R. Lea

Society for Research into Higher Education
& Open University Press

Open University Press
McGraw-Hill Education
McGraw-Hill House
Shoppenhangers Road
Maidenhead
Berkshire
England
SL6 2QL

email: enquiries@openup.co.uk
world wide web: www.openup.co.uk

and Two Penn Plaza, New York, NY 10121–2289, USA

First published 2007

A catalogue record of this book is available from the British Library

ISBN-13: 978 0 335 220878 (pb)   978 0 335 22088 5 (hb)
ISBN-10 0 335 220878 (pb)   0 335 22088 6 (hb)

Library of Congress Cataloging-in-Publication Data
CIP data has been applied for

Typeset by RefineCatch Limited, Bungay, Suffolk
Printed in Poland by OzGraf S.A.
www.polskabook.pl

The **McGraw·Hill** Companies

Contents

Acknowledgements

We would like to thank the following people for their help in providing both material for the case studies and examples we have used in this book, and the inspiration of their innovative work in the fields of language and e-learning: David Russell and David Fisher for the MyCase study; Julie Hughes and her students for the PGCE study; Marion Walton and Arlene Archer for the information about web literacy work and the Isiseko project at the University of Cape Town; Colleen McKenna for advice on the electronic literacy course at University College London; and Cathy Kell for pointing us to the Voyager website.

We would like to acknowledge the Higher Education Academy as the copyright holder and original publisher of the website page and text that we have reproduced in Figures 1.1 and 1.2 (pages 19–21), and Martin Dougiamas as the owner and original publisher of the Moodle website page that we have reproduced in Figure 4.0.

Thanks also to our publishers, Open University Press/McGraw-Hill, and to our colleagues in the Institute of Educational Technology and the Applied Language and Literacies Research Unit at the Open University for their collegiality and support.

Finally, I would like to make a personal acknowledgement to Steph Taylor for all she has done in support of my contribution to this book (RG).

Introduction

Robin Goodfellow and Mary R. Lea

This book is the result of research and collaboration between us as teachers, researchers and authors during the last seven years. In it we present a case for locating the concept and practice of e-learning within a language- and literacies-based approach to teaching and learning. We foreground the social practices of the university, its literacies and discourses and the ways in which these interplay with technologies. Our main objective has been to take a critical lens to what we see as the 'taken-for-granted' discourses of e-learning in the university and to propose an approach to learning and teaching with technologies which is based on an understanding of the processes of the production and consumption of texts in online education. As such, we aim to offer a unique approach to understanding e-learning and introduce the reader to a way of looking at this growing field which draws centrally on literacies research and practice. The book challenges the more dominant view of e-learning as a technology which can be separated off from the traditional concerns of the geographically located university, those of teaching and learning disciplinary-based bodies of knowledge. We question this approach, which valorizes the virtual and has the effect of decoupling universities from their histories and traditions, arguing that in order to understand these new environments for teaching and learning we need to look closely at the relationship between technologies, literacies and learning in specific pedagogical and disciplinary contexts.

We begin by introducing our own histories and academic trajectories. Issues of 'language in education' have formed a part of both of our journeys, albeit rather differently. Possibly as a result, finding ourselves in an environment where technology seemed increasingly to be the driver for educational development, we both began to ask questions about the taken-for-granted relationship between learning and technologies in higher education. In recognition of the fact that we bring our own particular academic and disciplinary backgrounds to this book, rather than attempt to create a unified authorial voice, we have decided to maintain sole authorship for some of the chapters; others we feel have been more valuably authored jointly. To help locate these contrasting but complementary perspectives, we each provide below a brief biographical journey.

Mary

This particular journey began some twenty years ago when I first taught English as a foreign language (EFL) to adult learners. My classroom experience of the ways in which issues of culture were so central to language learning and translation, led to my taking an MA in Applied Linguistics at the University of Sussex. Through my studies, I began to understand much more about how discourses worked as expressions of the relationship between language and society. Simultaneously, I was fortunate to be able to take-up a research assistant post, at what was then the Polytechnic of North London, researching what faculty members perceived as problems and difficulties with student writing. It soon became apparent that the traditional ways of talking about student writing, using linguistic-based descriptors of writing problems (grammar, syntax, spelling and punctuation), only scratched at the surface of the kinds of difficulties that students were experiencing. There were clearly major hurdles for those from non-traditional academic backgrounds to cross in their engagement with academic discourses and unfamiliar ways of talking about new kinds of knowledge (Lea 1994). In 1995 Brian Street (whose work on literacies as social practice was already seminal in the study of literacies) and I, were awarded an Economic and Social Research Council grant to study academic literacies in two contrasting university contexts. Our research findings pointed to significant gaps between student and tutor[1] expectations around writing at university and also highlighted the range and diversity of literacy practices that students were required to engage in for assessment as they moved between disciplines, subjects, courses, departments and even individual tutors (Lea and Street 1998). Following my appointment as a research fellow at the Open University (OU), a new research project with students studying at a distance, showed remarkably similar findings concerning students' struggles with the often implicit and shifting ground rules of academic literacies (Lea 1998). At the same time, based as I was in the Institute of Educational Technology, I became increasingly aware of the fact that attention to technologies was beginning to dominate discussions around learning. Curiously, though, these paid little, if any, attention to the writing that was going on in student and tutor interactions in these new electronic environments for learning. Consequently, my subsequent research began to look in some depth at the intersection between literacies, learning and technologies and what this might be able to tell us about the ways in which institutional practices were being played out within these new

---

[1] Throughout this book we use the word 'tutor' in its UK sense to refer to any academic member of staff taking a teaching role.

technologically mediated learning environments (Lea 2000, 2001, 2004a, 2005).

Robin

My journey began in the 1970s, teaching English and drama in East London secondary schools, it was there that I learned my first lessons in the role of social power in the management (and disruption) of learning. Later I too became involved in teaching EFL, at a time when pedagogy in that field was moving away from concern with structural models of language (grammar, syntax, spelling and pronunciation) towards a 'communicative approach' which foregrounded the different ways that meanings are negotiated in social contexts. Ironically, it was in this intensely interpersonal discourse environment that I first encountered the use of computers for learning, a strangely myopic activity back in those days of green text on black screens and drill-and-practice programs. But the promise of independent learning and increased teacher productivity offered by the use of computers weighed strongly in the commercial world of EFL, and I found myself being encouraged to learn to program and to explore the possibility of constructing dialogues between learner and machine that would allow the learner to acquire language at the same time as they were able to play with a new and increasingly fascinating electronic toy. The fascination led me first into an MSc course in Artificial Intelligence, at what was then Kingston Polytechnic, then into a series of publicly funded research projects in computer-assisted language learning, and finally into the OU's Institute of Educational Technology, first as a PhD student, and then as a lecturer in new technologies in teaching. All the time I was seeking the holy grail of a computer program that could interact with a human learner sufficiently engagingly to be a cause of their learning. By the time the Internet, in the form of the World Wide Web, burst on the educational scene in the 1990s, however, I had discovered enough about distance education to realize that formal learning is too complex and too important for learners to be entrusted to engagement with materials or technologies, however ingeniously they may be designed. I had also begun to realize that this was not a view necessarily shared by governmental and corporate drivers of educational policy servicing the 'knowledge economy', and that debates were emerging, among students and between students and teachers on the courses I worked on, and among my teaching, research and development colleagues, over the proper role of electronically mediated practices in the shaping of the learning experience. My own research began to focus on an examination of the institutional realities behind pedagogical practices which were being constructed as 'innovative' and 'transformational' by the e-learning community of which I was part, but which seemed to me to be as likely to involve their participants in struggles over status and voice almost as intense as those I had experienced as a secondary school teacher (Goodfellow 2001, 2004b, 2006; Goodfellow *et al.* 2001).

Literacies and technologies: reflections and definitions

As we have indicated earlier, we believe that adopting a mixed approach to authoring this book – some chapters together, some separately – has been the most effective way to present our arguments and to remain true to our own contrasting disciplinary and practice histories, with their associated epistemologies. In addition, we are particularly keen to speak to a range of practitioners: educational developers; educational technologists; e-learning specialists; subject teachers; literacies researchers; and, e-learning researchers. This reflects the eclectic nature of this field, where readers are drawn from wide-ranging disciplinary and practice contexts. We feel that the approach we have adopted in authoring this book will help this process, with particular chapters being possibly more 'user friendly' for some readers than for others. We believe that if we had tried to create a seamless text with one unified voice we would not have been able to do justice to the distinctive perspectives we have brought to this book. One authoritative voice would inevitably have silenced our individual ones, something we wanted to avoid, not only because this would have limited the scope for the variety of theoretical and methodological frameworks informing our argument, but also because we would have fallen short of addressing what we hope will be a wide range of readers. In authoring both separately and together, we hope that we have been able to do justice to a complex field which draws into the same conversation a number of underlying frameworks from studies of language, technologies and literacies. As a result, the chapters reflect our own different styles and approaches. They also operate at both the macro and the micro level, with some chapters looking at the detail of texts and others taking a broader critical approach.

Studies of literacies, in different educational contexts, have provided us with empirical and ethnographically grounded rich descriptions of practice (Street 1984; Barton and Hamilton 1998). In this book we bring together a number of related fields of inquiry which all take as their starting point a concern with literacies as social and cultural practice; these are variously described as New Literacy Studies (Heath 1983; Street 1984; Cook-Gumperz 1986; Gee 1992; Barton 1994), multiliteracies (New London Group 1996; Cope and Kalantzis 1999; Kress 2003b), techno- or silicon-literacies (Lankshear *et al.* 2000; Snyder 2002) or academic literacies (Ivanič 1998; Lea and Street 1998, 1999; Lillis 2001). We use the framing they offer us to ask questions about the 'newness' of literacies and texts, and their association to technologies and institutional practice, and in order to explore further the relationship between literacies and technologies. Although our focus is on e-learning contexts, we recognize that there is nothing new about the association of technologies with literacies. Technologies are always present when we explore literacies in educational contexts and, therefore, any theory of literacy as social practice always takes account of them. However, whereas the more familiar one of pen and paper have become invisible to us, focusing on the 'newness' of technologies may blind us to the embedded social and cultural context of text production.

It may help the reader if, at this stage, we introduce some working definitions of the two key terms that are used throughout this book and whose relationship forms a central tenet of the arguments being rehearsed.

We are using the term *e-learning* to describe the explicit association of learning in tertiary education with electronic and digital applications and environments. This includes pretty much any learning in which a computer or other digital interface is involved: interactive multimedia programs; online discussion forums; web browsing and web link sharing tools; course announcement pages; chat rooms; course management systems; digital portfolios and the use of virtual learning environments (VLEs) for both pedagogical purposes and the institutional management of learning. At the time of writing, what most educationists regard as e-learning mainly involves the use of online interpersonal communication and the Internet as an information and publishing resource. We focus our discussion, therefore, on these particular practices, taking them as representative of all forms of learning which involve the composing and editing of digital texts.

Turning to *literacies*, a dictionary definition would tell us that literacy is concerned with the ability to read and write. Throughout this book we use the plural term 'literacies' in explicit contrast to the singular. Literacy in the singular implies a skill associated with learning and/or a cognitive activity which resides in and with the individual learner. In common with many literacies theorists whose work we draw upon in this book, we regard literacy as engagement in a range of socially and culturally situated practices which vary in terms of any particular context. In order to denote this complexity the plural form is used. Literacy is not a unitary skill which, once learnt, can be transferred with ease from context to context. Literacies take on a particular significance and form depending on the social relationships between the participants involved in a specific context and the texts which are involved. Importantly, literacies embed relationships of power and authority and are concerned with who has the right to write (or read), what can be written about and who makes these decisions. Writing and reading texts always embed these kinds of relationships and this is how and why some texts become more important, powerful and significant than others at any particular time within an institutional context.

These two terms are, of course, explored more fully in relation to other literature in the course of the following chapters.

An overview of the following chapters

In Chapter 1, Mary provides a framing for the chapters which follow in exploring the background against which e-learning is becoming a dominant frame for teaching and learning in higher education. In particular, she focuses on some of the discourses of learning evident in today's higher education and how e-learning is implicated within them. In order to do this she draws on the work of discourse analysts whose methodological contribution enables us to understand how language and discourses work in society in both constructing and reinforcing particular beliefs about the world and 'how things are'. Through an exploration of some university and government funded websites, Mary looks at the ways in which beliefs about learning are presented through institutional web pages and downloadable documentation. Drawing on examples, from the UK, she examines how the notion of learning is being reconfigured through the language of policy documents and their close alignment with documentation around e-learning, arguing that these are frequently being decoupled from disciplinary knowledge. In contrast, Mary provides an historical account of approaches to student learning which have been more closely tied to engagement with disciplinary knowledge. She also introduces a body of work which puts writing and texts at the heart of learning, setting the scene for further detailed discussion of this framing in Chapter 4. In paying increased attention to writing and the production of texts in the learning process, Mary concludes by suggesting that present-day research, in the field of writing development which foregrounds social and linguistic practices in meaning-making, offers a major contribution to our understanding of e-learning.

In Chapter 2, Robin argues for a conceptual move away from the metaphor of technologies as tools for learning towards thinking about technologies as sites of teaching and learning practice, a framing which highlights the social relations which come into play around learning. He provides an historical mapping of the ways in which computers have come to play a part in educational contexts and, in particular, how they have been associated with cognitive models of learning and constructivist and social constructivist pedagogies. This has paved the way for conceptualizations of online collaborative learning and learning communities which foreground the idea of interaction as key to learning with technologies. He argues, however, that this way of conceptualizing learning has not resolved contradictions that arise from the interaction of institutional priorities around assessment and accreditation with the principles of participation in learning communities. He suggests that technological environments, in which written communication is mainly shaped by institutional and academic relations of authority and social power, should be considered as sites of literacy practice rather than of interpersonal interaction.

In Chapter 3, Robin develops further the notion of technologies as sites of practice in which activity and meaning-making are shaped by the social relations derived from the wider social and institutional setting within which educational interaction is played out. He uses this perspective in order to explore the broader social and ideological dimensions in which university teaching and learning and the use of e-learning technologies operate. In particular, he examines the role of ideas about literacy in shaping the way we think about learning and communicating with technologies. He explores the notion that, despite their obvious electronic configuration, VLEs can be usefully considered as sites of institutional practice, located within a particular university context. Robin also locates present-day discussions of students as 'digital natives' within broader debates around a 'literacy crisis'. He offers a critical examination of the move from print to screen and the literacies which are associated with this shift, focusing specifically in this chapter upon the perspectives offered by multiliteracies and, more recently, the related 'new media' literacies theorists. He discusses Internet communication practices that are emerging around the Web 2.0 generation of web services and the social media sites they support, and critiques the view that these represent 'new' literacies that are being incorporated into academic practice. Robin makes a case for stimulating awareness and discussion around the mutual shaping of literacies and digital communication in the university, suggesting that paying attention to critical digital literacies should be central to all e-learning pedagogy and practice.

In Chapter 4, Mary asks questions about what it means to read and write as a student in the university and the implications of this for e-learning practice. The chapter draws its methodological framing from research in academic literacies, suggesting that this offers a useful tool for examining a more contested view of online learning than that provided by the constructivist framework which tends to dominate the e-learning field. Mary argues that in order to understand more about meaning-making and online learning we need to pay particular attention to specific texts and their associated practices, focusing on these interactions as sites of contestation and meaning-making and not necessarily as benign, as a collaborative learning model might suggest. She also takes issue with the tendency for literacies theorists to focus on mode and, in particular, on the 'newness' of multimodal texts. She argues that what typifies the genres associated with new media in higher education is not primarily their multimodality but their nature as forms of writing and the social relations and practices around this writing. Mary reminds us that, whatever the context, acts of reading and writing are never neutral; they are always mediated by particular contexts and embed relationships of power and authority. She provides examples of e-learning practices around texts as evidence that they are never separated off from deeper concerns about how knowledge is made and who has the power and authority over that knowledge. Overall, she makes the case for the contribution that academic literacies, with its focus on the texts of learning, can make to informing some general principles of use for practitioners in e-learning contexts.

The jointly authored Chapter 5 introduces a number of different case studies which we argue are paying attention to the nature of literacies as integral to e-learning environments, even though the university teachers whose courses we draw upon may be using related rather than identical theoretical and methodological frames to ours in situating their pedagogic approach. We begin by providing an illustration of a rationalist and skills-focused perspective in practice, in the context of what has come to be termed 'information literacy'. We critique this viewpoint by contrasting it with three examples of approaches to teaching which are informed by a literacies perspective. We then go on to present detailed accounts of two further teaching contexts, one from the USA and one from the UK, in which a similar social literacies perspective has been applied to pedagogy in the specific curriculum areas of teacher education and biosystems engineering. We believe that these cases illustrate the general principles of our literacies perspective in action in pedagogic contexts and also support our argument that this is a challenge for e-learning across the board, not only for areas where there is already a formal interest in text. The courses we refer to reflect a range of subjects, levels, professional/academic epistemologies, and use of technologies, and are drawn from institutions across the anglophone academic world. At the end of the chapter we consider the implications for promoting the kind of teaching and learning practices that these exemplify for educational development across the higher education sector.

In Chapter 6, also jointly authored, we address emerging e-learning practices in the areas of 'open courseware' and the use of electronic portfolios, which we see as embedding a tension between the institutional goal of managing learning, and the broader social ideal of learner empowerment. We examine some of the issues raised by the free availability of high-quality but decontextualized teaching material and the introduction of digital portfolios. We explore these in terms of the relationship between disciplinary and practice-based knowledge, assessment and the possibilities for user-generated content, the authoring and editing of texts. We explore the ways in which the university sector itself is harnessing e-learning to develop new genres of learning texts through, for example, personal development planning. Using the example of an online course at our own institution, we explore some of the hybrid texts and complex practices that students bring to e-portfolio work, and the issues that these raise for teachers and students who are more familiar with conventional academic practices. We bring the book to a conclusion by critiquing some of the existing research in e-learning and pointing to the urgent need for further work which brings literacies research into alignment with approaches to digital learning.

1

Approaches to learning: developing e-learning agendas

Mary R. Lea

This chapter provides a framing for those which follow in paying particular attention to the context within which e-learning is becoming one of the dominant paradigms for teaching and learning worldwide in the twenty-first century. It examines the role assigned to new technologies not only in relation to curriculum and pedagogy but also in the broader remit of the university in terms of its perceived societal and commercial role in the global knowledge economy. In a close analysis of some policy agendas around e-learning, it sets the scene for exploring how these are being taken up in the repositioning of universities in the global marketplace and the concurrent marginalization of teaching and learning of a traditional academic curriculum concerned with disciplinary-based knowledge. In so doing, it draws upon some language-based approaches which provide the tools for exploring a critical analysis of many of the teaching and learning practices which are becoming associated with the e-learning paradigm, foregrounding how language works in implicitly constructing particular formations of the educational world. This is a theme which is picked up throughout this book in different ways, as we draw on theoretical frameworks provided by various studies and research into language and literacies. It is possible that this approach might not meet the standards of analytical rigour and critical discussion that some language specialists might wish to apply. Equally, it may not be perceived by some educational developers as having any particular relevance to their day-to-day practice. In the broad field of language in education, within which this book sits, this tension is one which is continually coming to the fore. The intention is that this chapter, and the book more generally, will go some way to addressing this, in providing a pathway which makes linguistic and literacies-based research and theory more accessible to educational practitioners in other domains and also makes higher educational practice more visible to research and theory in studies of language and literacies. I believe that the merging of these two domains, educational practice and literacies research, is an ongoing challenge for those of us in higher educational development who are drawing on these interdisciplinary concepts and approaches in our writing but whose main concern is to provide principles for practice, rather than to contribute to theorized debates around language. The orientation of this chapter is, in part, a response to this challenge.

Methodological considerations

My concern here is with the discourses of learning in higher education and their reconfiguration in terms of e-learning agendas. The general approach I adopt is framed by the work of applied linguists who have contributed a valuable understanding of the ways in which language and discourses work in society (Fairclough 1992; Blommaert 2005; Gee 2005). For those readers who are interested in a critical overview of some relevant approaches to discourse analysis and broader social structures, Blommaert (2005) provides a highly accessible overview. Although the concept of discourse has been taken up in different ways across the social sciences, as a discipline linguistics tends to lay most claim to the study of language. However, as Blommaert (2005) argues, linguistic features alone are not enough to tell us what is going on in the study of texts; it is always 'language in action' that defines discourses, so that we always need to situate a particular discourse in its social, cultural and historical context in order for it to be fully understood. This includes not just the more conventional aspects of language studied by linguists but what Blommaert (2005: 3) refers to as 'all forms of meaningful semiotic human activity seen in connection with social, cultural and historical patterns and developments of use'. Blommaert's definition reflects the increasing interest in multimodality and the broader semiotic domain in the new communicative order (Kress and van Leeuwen 2001; Kress 2003b) and the whole field of learning, literacies and technologies which is the concern of this book more generally (see, in particular, Chapter 3 for further discussion).

Gee (2000) outlines how, by the end of the last century, the social and linguistic turn had become well-established within the social sciences. Increasingly central to these developments, has been a focus on the social and cultural characteristics of discourses in their historical contexts as powerful ways of both talking and writing in relation to broader social and institutional practices. I draw on this perspective later in this chapter when exploring how the circulation of both written and visual texts, in web pages and policy documents, has become associated with views of learning which have become normalized and, increasingly, apparently uncontestable within higher education. Gee (2005) also explores how, working within discourse, language always has a dual function in both constructing and reflecting the situation or contexts in which it is used. In other words, the more we use language and discourses in particular kinds of ways, the more something comes into being as a common-sense way of how things are. This is particularly the case in institutional and political contexts where different stakeholders are jostling for position and authority, drawing upon rhetorical resources to project a particular view of the world, such as that represented by the new agendas of e-learning with which this book is concerned. In common with Blommaert, Gee (2005) also focuses on language in action and the ways in which language is called into play in enacting particular social activities in different institutional contexts. He highlights how one particularly important element of the ways in which language works is that of 'intertextuality'. Intertextuality refers to the ways in which other texts are always brought into play when language is used, either implicitly or explicitly. This is evident in the exploration, below, in relation to the discourses and dominant rhetorical stances which are being played out in e-learning and educational agendas. Alluding to other texts evokes a particular kind of world; I examine below how this is happening within this context and the general reconfiguration of higher education.

Policy documents have for some time been recognized by critical discourse analysts as embedding and reinforcing particular understandings (Fairclough 2000). More recently the development of the Web has enabled authoritative bodies, such as universities, government departments and funding agencies, to publicize and foreground their own policy documents, which are readily edited and updated and, crucially, linked to other similar websites. In this way discourses around educational policy can become widespread and dominant, and others, which provide alternative viewpoints, marginalized. Through exploring websites, such as those considered below, we can see how beliefs about learning and technologies are reinforced, despite the fact that these may not necessarily mirror the lived experience of either academics or students in today's universities. In fact, we know very little about the actual implications of e-learning agendas for learners, despite the fact that there has been a rapid growth in appointments to posts within universities which have been designed to promote e-learning and the use of technologies across the curriculum. In a climate in which a celebratory rhetoric heralds each new iteration of technologies as transforming the learning experience, this chapter examines how learning itself is being subtly realigned within this new agenda.

Changes in higher education

In providing some background to the analysis which follows, I turn now to the last decade of the twentieth century, which saw profound changes in tertiary education as universities worldwide began to respond to a global market. Universities which had traditionally looked within their own national boundaries for student recruitment were required increasingly to refashion themselves as commercial, market-led organizations, a trend which has become known as the commodification of higher education; what Noble (2002) describes as 'the conversion of intellectual activity into commodity form' in order to render it a commercial good. In addition to providing tertiary education for increasing numbers of domestic students, the market-ization of the sector resulted in the enrolment of more students from over-seas. At the same time, in the UK at least, government initiatives were being put in place to support widening participation for groups of students who had been previously underrepresented in higher education. Changes in the student body were accompanied by changes in the curriculum and redefi-nitions of what constituted degree-level study. Vocational and professional subjects were drawn into the university curriculum, leading to degrees in a range of fields, such as nursing, occupational therapy and business studies, which had previously relied upon 'on the job' training. Changes were also taking place in the traditional academic curriculum, with the introduction of modular courses in which assumptions could no longer be made about the entry-level knowledge of students or their path of progression through a discipline (Davidson and Lea 1994). In part as a result of these moves towards modularization, interdisciplinary study, for example, courses in environmental studies, sports sciences and media studies, became increas-ingly popular with students, competing with more traditional disciplines and subjects, such as history, economics and chemistry, for space in faculty degree programmes.

Accompanying these profound changes in the sector, increased attention began to be paid to issues of teaching and learning in higher education. In the UK these were largely the result of the recommendations of the National Committee of Inquiry into Higher Education (NCIHE 1997). This commit-tee, chaired by Sir Ronald Dearing, was set up to report on the state of the UK university sector. What became known as the Dearing Report made a number of recommendations, the implementation of which resulted in far-reaching changes to the face of higher education. These included giving high priority to developing and implementing learning, and teaching strat-egies which would focus specifically on the promotion of students' learning. In addition, it suggested that all institutions of higher education be charged with immediately offering programmes for teacher training of their staff, which included paying particular attention to issues of teaching and learn-ing. Prior to Dearing, most training for university teachers in the UK had taken place only in those higher education institutions which focused upon teaching, as opposed to those more traditional universities which focused primarily upon research. As a result of the procedures put in place by the Dearing Report, accreditation for all new teachers in UK higher education is now taking place across the sector, with almost all higher education institu-tions providing their own accredited individual programmes of training. The Institute for Learning and Teaching in Higher Education was also set up as a consequence of Dearing, in order to oversee the national accreditation of such programmes. This was later reconstituted as the Higher Education Academy (HEA), which, in addition, has been charged with commissioning research into learning and teaching practices and with stimulating innova-tion in the area. Further recommendations made by the report have been implemented in the requirement for programmes of study to clearly identify outcomes, in terms of skills and understanding, and their relationship to the world of work. All in all, the Dearing Report set the stage for a comprehensive and radical shake-up of higher education linking it much more directly than ever before to the development of the knowledge economy.

Developments in new technologies

At the same time that issues of teaching and learning were beginning to be taken seriously, new technologies were being explored enthusiastically by universities, in part because from the mid-1990s their implementation was linked to generous government funding for technology-led initiatives. Such programmes were operationalized in different ways, depending on the national context. For example, in Australia the concept of 'flexible learning' was seen as the key to responding to changing conditions of higher education with the provision of a market-oriented mass system. According to Garrick and Jakupec (2000: 3):

> Flexible learning is seen by education and training institutions . . . as a vehicle for addressing current economic, social, political, technological and cultural issues caused by the forces of globalization. That is, globalization has made it imperative for education and training organizations and public and private enterprise to develop more flexible approaches to learning. This includes new approaches to course planning, structures, delivery methods and access to education, training and staff development.

In the Australian case early funding around the use of technologies in higher education was targeted towards supporting 'flexible learning', often in dual campus contexts delivering both face-to-face and distance education from the same institution. In contrast, although in the UK distance education was the first to begin to make use of educational technologies in any substantial way, much of the initial UK funding for the use of new technologies was targeted towards traditional campus-based universities. In fact, as early as 1992 the Universities Funding Council launched the first phase of its Teaching and Learning Technology Programme, which made available £7.5 million per year over three years, in order for universities to develop new methods of teaching and learning through the use of technology. Forty-three projects were funded under this first phase, and a second phase, funding a further 33 projects, began in 1993, this time funded by the now newly established higher education funding councils in England (HEFCE), Scotland, Wales and Northern Ireland.

These initiatives – further reinforced by the recommendations of the Dearing Report that all university staff be trained and supported in the use of what was referred to at the time as 'communications and information technology' – ensured that new technologies became seen as central to the delivery of higher education. More specifically, technologies were regarded as crucial to making possible a curriculum which in principle could be accessed anytime and anywhere, arguably providing the possibility of decoupling it from institutions and operating more effectively within a global higher education. This shake-up in higher education, and the movement from a local and national to a global market, has resulted in an uneasy juxtaposition of the old and the new for many universities. At the same time as positioning themselves in the global higher education market, some of the most established universities also rely upon their located and physical history as high-status academic institutions in order to operate effectively within the marketplace. One such example is visible on the website of University College London (UCL); this is a prestigious institution, one of the UK's leading research universities. Describing itself as 'London's Global University', it foregrounds its international strategy thus:

> UCL has an ambitious agenda to ensure that its students are capable of helping those in need around the world, and to provide an education that ensures that its students become global citizens.
>   Speaking to 'The Independent', Professor Michael Worton, Vice-Provost of UCL (Academic & International), described the university's intent to transform itself into a global university. The article quotes from UCL's new International Strategy: 'As a result of a combination of globalization, the development of new technologies and, in the UK, the shift from an elite to a mass higher education system, higher education is undergoing what amounts to a revolution. It is important for UCL to recognize the magnitude of what is happening and to embrace the opportunity to change itself radically.'
> (http://www.ucl.ac.uk/news-archive/for-ucl/latest/
> newsitem.shtml?05010110, accessed March 2007)

Nevertheless, despite this explicit recognition of the changing nature of higher education, and moves towards a mass system fuelled in part by the introduction of new technologies, UCL still relies on very traditional representations of student life in order to present itself to the wider world. Following a link from the university's home page, it is possible to access web pages which are specifically concerned with teaching and learning:

> These pages not only provide the resources necessary to ensure consistent delivery and assessment of teaching at UCL but they also direct students towards the resources necessary to ensure that they are properly prepared to undertake purposeful and successful learning.
> (http://www.ucl.ac.uk/teaching-learning, accessed March 2007)

In contrast to the emphasis on radical change for the university in a global world suggested in its international strategy above, the visual images chosen to present UCL globally evoke a world far removed from the market-oriented, technologically focused shift to a mass system. Across the centre of one of the web pages there are three photographs which take up a large proportion of the screen. Presumably, the display of these three different images is intended to represent aspects of being a student at UCL. The photograph on the left is of an entrance to one of the university's Victorian buildings in central London; on the right a photograph shows the rear of a similarly aged building, this time foregrounded and framed by Virginia creeper growing on the walls of the college building, giving a city garden feel. In the central position is a photograph of a group of students in university gowns and mortar boards; the photo has been taken from behind and the broader setting has been cropped so that all that is visible are the rear views of nine unidentified students. The way in which this photograph is displayed, located between two other photographs of UCL's Victorian buildings and gardens in central London, is clearly meant to evoke a very traditional learning experience in a capital city at a prestigious institution. This public website is a useful representation of the tension within universities between the traditional curriculum offerings to students and the newness of the global market and its associated technologies. There is no intention here to single UCL out in the way in which images and text on the website juxtapose different readings of 'the university' in today's higher education. Its website is used here only as a valuable example of the ways in which very different, and in many ways conflicting, understandings of higher education are juxtaposed on university websites throughout the world and provide the broader context for discussions around e-learning. Bayne's (2006) observation that university crests almost always embody some representation of the printed word, for example, the bound book, even when these crests are being used to present a university's virtual presence, provides further evidence for the ways in which the different readings of the physically located and virtual global university rub up against one another.

Exploring accounts of e-learning

One thread which runs throughout this book is an approach which takes a critical lens to the ways in which higher education is being reconfigured through the implementation of a technological agenda as a key component of today's market-oriented higher education. In order to provide more contextualization of the ways in which agendas are played out, I turn now to some contemporary accounts of both student learning more generally and e-learning in particular. Since this is the context with which I am most familiar, I continue to draw my examples from the UK but would encourage the reader to conduct similar explorations in their own particular context.

Contemporary accounts of e-learning are not difficult to explore since the Web provides ready access to official sites which are concerned with its development and support. In the UK there are a number of related government-funded bodies which hold responsibility for implementing e-learning policies; these are the higher education funding councils, for England, Scotland, Wales and Northern Ireland, the Joint Information Systems Committee (JISC) and the HEA. There is an integral relationship between these bodies, but it is the JISC which appears to hold the major responsibility for the practical implementation of policies concerning the use of new technologies. In October 2004 it described its activities as 'working with further and higher education in providing strategic guidance, advice and opportunities to use information and communication technologies (ICT) to support teaching, learning, research and administration' (http://www.jisc.ac.uk/dfes_elearning.html accessed October 2004). It would be wrong to assume that this meant it took a deterministic view of technology with respect to supporting learning. Indeed, its response to the Department of Education and Science policy on e-learning on its website, in June 2004, in March was to caution that it would be a mistake to treat e-learning as a single entity and also a mistake to assume that e-learning was automatically a good thing. Further, the JISC response acknowledged that the value of e-learning is wholly dependent on the purpose for which it is applied and the successful achievement of the intended outcomes.

It is perhaps useful to pause here and provide some background to this discussion which is, in fact, pertinent to its exploration. The earliest draft of the present chapter was written in September 2004, when I accessed a number of detailed pages on the JISC website which outlined its response to the Department of Education and Science e-learning strategy. The prominence accorded to the JISC response, on its own website, at that time, appeared to suggest that this was an important indication of JISC policy towards the use of new technologies in teaching and learning, particularly with respect to some mitigation towards the supposed benefits of e-learning, as indicated above. However, by mid-2006 it was no longer possible to access any of the web pages which made reference to this particular response; the mitigation had, therefore, effectively disappeared. In addition, the page at http://www.jisc.ac.uk/dfes_elearning.html (accessed in October 2004), which had provided a description of the JISC role (see above), had also disappeared from the site to be replaced by a new statement of its mission as 'to provide world-class leadership in the innovative use of Information and Communications Technology to support education and research' (http://www.jisc.ac.uk accessed March 2007). Links from this page take one to further statements on the JISC's role. There is of course nothing unusual in the redesign and building of websites and the removal of out-of-date material. Nevertheless, when these sites are primarily concerned with the implementation of government-funded policy around education we need to be mindful of their rhetorical power in enabling the easy and accessible presentation of particular and powerful representations of the educational landscape. Removing important documents and visible responses to them has the immediate effect of redefining agendas and promoting perspectives which, by the omission of other previously retrievable web-based material, then become dominant. Questions and discussions around educational practice, learning and technologies become harder to maintain when sites are permanently redesigned to present homogeneity.

The JISC response to the e-learning strategy mirrored that of HEFCE whose own 'Strategy for e-learning', published in 2005 and still accessible in January 2007 from http://www.hefce.ac.uk/news/hefce/2005/elearning.htm, suggests that:

> E-learning has been criticised for being technology led, with a focus on providing materials, but has recently focused more on the learner and enabling students and other users to develop more independence in learning and to share resources. This change matches the developments in pedagogy and the increasing need to support diversity and flexibility in higher education.
>
> (HEFCE, *et al.* 2005: 4)

Although the introduction of new technologies in 1990s was frequently accompanied by deterministic rhetoric championing a simple relationship between the use of new technologies and 'better learning', there has been a gradual move away from this position towards recognition of the implications for learners of using these technologies (see Chapter 2 for further discussion). This perspective is carried forward in the HEFCE strategy, which aims:

> to integrate e-learning into higher education . . . to transform the learning experiences of students . . . including curriculum design, networked learning, student support, strategic management, quality, research and evaluation, and infrastructure.
>
> (http://www.hefce.ac.uk/news/hefce/2005/elearning.htm accessed March 2007)

This foregrounding of e-learning and its relationship to the student learning experience, and therefore, one would assume, attention to issues of pedagogy, is worthy of note and warrants a more thorough exploration. Indeed, it is this relationship between the twin goals of 'integrating e-learning into higher education' and 'transforming the learning experience of students' that we are concerned to unpack in this book, suggesting that the literacies perspective developed in subsequent chapters allows us to throw new light on the ways in which the second goal is being operationalized in practice contexts.

Perhaps tellingly, the HEFCE strategy makes no explicit mention of learning in relation to subject and disciplinary bodies of knowledge: academic, professional or vocational. Instead the 'student experience' seems to be an overarching descriptor which includes aspects of what could be more accurately described as the 'university experience' but not directly that of learning academic content. The HEFCE definition presents a very particular discourse of 'learning', primarily one which is concerned with issues of quality, skills and outcomes – the net effect being to construct a description of learning in higher education with which most educational developers will be all too familiar. It is useful, in a discussion of what constitutes 'learning' in higher education, to draw on the work of Fairclough (1992), who reminds us of the power of language and its ability to make things seem like common sense through embedding particular presuppositions, which become the very 'way things are' and in this way serve to build ideologies:

> I shall understand ideologies to be significations/constructions of reality (the physical world, social relations, social identities), which are built into various dimensions of the forms/meanings of discursive practices ... The ideologies embedded in discursive practices are most effective when they become naturalized, and achieve the status of common sense.
>
> (Fairclough 1992: 87)

Whereas twenty years ago it would have been very unusual to find publications concerned with student learning which were not based on implicit understandings about the academic business of teaching subjects and disciplines, we are now so familiar with the discourses found at an instant on websites, such as those described above, that they warrant very little reaction from the reader. Notwithstanding, I argue that we need to be cautious about the ways in which these web pages and their accompanying policy documents embed particular 'ways of knowing', particular taken-for-granted assumptions about what is meant by learning in relation to higher education.

The learning experience: supporting learning

In order to find out more about student learning, I turned to the website of the HEA; this government-funded body was formed in May 2004 from a merger of the Institute for Learning and Teaching in Higher Education, the Learning and Teaching Support Network, and the Teaching Quality Enhancement Fund National Co-ordination Team, apparently as a result of a review of the arrangements for supporting the enhancement of quality in learning and teaching in higher education. These formations and regroupings have become the outward manifestation of official government-funded policies and their associated discourses around learning. At present, the HEA's stated mission is 'to help institutions, discipline groups and all staff to provide the best possible learning experience for their students'. (http://www.heacademy.ac.uk accessed March 2007).

Figure 1.1 provides a visual overview of the pages of the HEA website which are concerned with supporting learning. It is here that I expected to find discussions about student learning both in relation to and separate from the use of new technologies. The site is divided into eight topics: assessment; curriculum; e-learning; employability and enterprise; learning and teaching; quality; student support; and, widening participation. Following the links from each topic heading provides an explanation of the particular concerns addressed in each of these areas. These are reproduced in full in Figure 1.2 since the detail is particularly pertinent to the argument.

The topic descriptions provide some indication of the ways in which the HEA conceptualizes what is involved in 'supporting learning'. This appears

Figure 1.1 Overview of the HEA website

to be primarily in terms of processes and policy at the institutional level. For example, the topic of e-learning is primarily constructed as an institutional and stakeholder activity, with an emphasis on strategy. The use of acronyms, such as CETLs and ALT, assume the reader is already familiar with a particular discourse and that there is a self-evident relationship between the different bodies concerned with e-learning, that is, HEA, JISC and HEFCE. Since all three websites' e-learning pages refer backwards and forwards to one another, what we find is that all these government-funded bodies are creating a particular perspective through links to each other's sites and policy documents. It is useful to remember here the discussions around language earlier in this chapter and, in particular, how alluding to other texts, through implicit and explicit intertextual reference, reinforces particular beliefs about the world. In this instance, this has the effect of strengthening the dominance of a particular model of learning and its

Assessment of learning
Higher education faces many concerns and contradictions in its pursuit of effective practice in learning, teaching and assessment. Assuring quality is increasingly important but certification can predominate with consequent disadvantages to student learning. In response to these and other issues the Higher Education Academy produces resources and co-ordinates a number of activities to share and embed effective practice.

Curriculum
Curriculum development is an important and challenging process. We support institutions and their staff in this process by providing resources, undertaking research and organizing events.
Internationalization and sustainability are two areas of growing importance with implications for curriculum.

e-Learning
We acknowledge the need for an holistic approach to embedding e-learning in institutional activities. It aims to address the real needs of institutions and their stakeholders in order to facilitate the implementation of effective strategies and practices. To achieve these aims we are working closely with key stakeholders including the Heads of e-Learning Forum (HeLF), relevant CETLs, ALT, the Leadership Foundation and the JISC.
Central to the Academy's e-learning activities is the implementation, in collaboration with the JISC, of HEFCE's e-learning Strategy, building on current collaborative work with the JISC, e.g. through the Distributed eLearning Programme.
The HEFCE e-Learning Strategy is available for download at http://www.hefce.ac.uk/pubs/hefce/2005/05_12/

Employability and enterprise
These pages are populated with useful information and resources to support you and your colleagues to effectively understand and engage with employability. They were jointly produced by the Higher Education Academy and the Enhancing Student Employability Skills Co-ordination Team (ESECT)
You can use the right hand navigation bar to find out more and access a variety of information, tools and resources.

Learning and Teaching
Much of the work of the Higher Education Academy relates to responding to the changing support needs of the HE community arising from issues of both policy and practice in teaching and learning – how students are taught, by whom and with what relationship between the research and teaching roles of the academic community.
A key part of the student experience must relate to how they are taught and how they may be encouraged to reflect, evaluate and provide feedback upon their learning. The Academy is heavily involved in helping the sector to respond to the e-learning agenda, to build capacity for enquiry-based learning and to explore, share and embed effective student feedback practice. The extensive programme of work being co-ordinated on behalf of the Progress File Implementation Group continues the Academy's commitment to PDP as a core educational process for the realization of students' potential.
Likewise, helping institutions to address both the staff development needs consequent upon the changing ratio of full-time to part-time teachers and the issues relating to the development of postgraduates who teach is an area of work in which the Academy continues to be active.
Building the relationships between research and teaching also remains a central aim and recognizes an increasing interest in this area. Activity is designed to both contribute to and to stimulate debate, addressing both generic and discipline specific themes around the scholarship of teaching and learning.

Figure 1.2   Supporting learning – the HEA website

Quality

The Higher Education Academy seeks to work collaboratively with the sector to enhance the quality of the student experience.

Change Academy

We work with the Leadership Foundation for Higher Education to deliver Change Academy.

External Examining

We have a multifaceted programme of research and development to support external examining. The Academy is working with many different interest groups to share practice, build knowledge, facilitate networking and create new programmes for the professional development of external examiners and higher education teachers who aspire to be the external examiners of tomorrow.

Quality Enhancement

We provide a forum for the discussion of quality enhancement issues – principles, practice and new developments – and a route for communication between academic practitioners, institutional managers and policy-makers.

Quality Management

This is one of the themes identified by higher education institutions as a principal area of interest for Academy support. The programme includes workshops, seminars and conferences with related publications and materials.

Student support

Everything we do is aimed at improving the student learning experience.

This focus leads us to work on all aspects of the student learning life cycle – including strategies for retention, the effective uses of e-learning, the development of enterprise capabilities, and support for excellent research training environments. Information on all of these activities can be found elsewhere on the website.

This section of the website focuses on a number of areas that directly support student learning: supporting students with disabilities, personal development planning and progress files, and personal tutoring.

Widening participation

We are committed to supporting institutions to widen participation and enhance the learning experience of students from all backgrounds. We do this by:

- Commissioning, undertaking and disseminating research to inform national, institutional and disciplinary policy and practice in relation to widening participation.
- The development of a directory of widening participation practice.
- Supporting work on personal tutoring.
- Establishing a widening participation research service to support the sector to make better use of existing research and information.

Figure 1.2 Continued

relationship to technologies, and, by its omissions, making less visible any alternative perspectives. The descriptor of the topic of 'learning and teaching' is concerned with the 'how' and the 'by whom' of learning and with broader considerations of institutional structure in terms of research and teaching, but there is no explicit reference in this topic description to the content of what is being learnt or taught. Both e-learning and personal development planning (PDP) are called into play in terms of supporting learning, the latter described as a 'core educational process' but there is no explanation of how this might be related to learning subject-based knowledge.

What appears to be evident from the HEA 'supporting learning' web pages is that the notion of 'learning' is, effectively, being decoupled from any notion of individual student engagement with subject and disciplinary bodies of knowledge. Academic subjects and disciplines are strangely absent in the overall mapping of supporting learning. While the HEA Subject Centres do provide disciplinary support in 24 subject areas, and their pages can be accessed by following the link to 'subject network' on the supporting learning page (see Figure 1.1), only one of the supporting learning topic pages provides a web link to the Subject Centres, and this is placed not under the heading of 'curriculum', as one might expect, but under 'widening participation'. Overall, institutional strategies and processes and the management of learning and teaching are foregrounded at the expense of attention to engagement in subject-based bodies of knowledge. This is not in any way intended as a criticism of the valuable work carried out by HEA, JISC or HEFCE, but it does raise important questions concerning what is implicit in the term 'learning' and how the use of this word embeds all sorts of other agendas which are closely linked to the development of e-learning. Looking in some detail at the ways in which 'learning' is referred to on websites and in policy documents, provides evidence that the term is increasingly concerned with managing the learner through systems and processes rather than supporting student learners in engagement with disciplinary and subject-based knowledge. E-learning plays a central role in a conceptualization which is less about the student learner in terms of engaging with academic content and more about mapping personal development; in essence managing learning and pedagogy are becoming conflated. This is closely tied to the use of VLEs, such as WebCT, Blackboard and Moodle, which provide dual-purpose sites for both pedagogic engagement and recording student progress and personal development planning. The implications of the merging of pedagogy and the management of learning, through the implementation of VLEs, are considered further in Chapters 3 and 6.

Exploring contemporary accounts of 'student learning'

The representation of supporting learning we have explored so far in this chapter, with its focus at the level of policy and delivery systems, is in marked contrast to the conceptualization of student learning offered by a well-established, primarily European and Australian, research tradition. From the late 1970s a body of influential work, based on what is known as the phenomenographic tradition, challenged more behavioural and transmission models of learning. It gained credence widely in the early days of educational development from the mid-1980s, when Marton *et al.* (1984) published an edited volume documenting details concerning students' experiences of learning. This perspective focused on individual students' conceptions of learning, concentrating in particular on a distinction between deep and surface approaches. Whereas surface learning was concerned with the memorization of facts and rote learning, deep learning was identified where students were thought to be making complex meaning from their studies. Gibbs (1994) outlines four premises on which the phenomenographic tradition was based. First, students learn in qualitatively different ways: their approach to their studies is either an intention to make sense, a deep approach, or an attempt to reproduce, a surface approach. Second, the outcomes of student learning are not only quantitatively different but also qualitatively different. That is, students understand things in different ways; it is not just a case of knowing more or less. Third, students understand learning and knowledge and what they are doing when they are learning in different ways over time; they develop different conceptions of learning. Finally, university teachers also understand what constitutes good learning in qualitatively different ways. The overall focus of this approach, then, was on the ways in which students make meaning from their learning and on fostering the conditions in university teaching and learning for the engagement in deep, rather than surface, learning. Although, on the whole, it was not concerned with marked differences between learning in particular disciplines, some research was carried out across different disciplinary contexts. Hounsell (1988), for example, looked in depth at the problems students encountered when confronted with the unfamiliar discourses of the university. He identified academic discourse as a particular kind of written world with its own conventions, and illustrated this through an exploration of the different conceptions of essay writing involved in the contrasting disciplines of history and psychology. A later addition to the framework outlined by Gibbs (1994) was the strategic approach, in which students adopted an organizational strategy, focusing on getting the best marks, paying particular attention to assessment criteria and to the particular preferences of their lecturers.

Although critiques have been levelled at research in the pheonomenographic tradition for its lack of engagement in the broader institutional context (Lea and Street 1998), its lack of fitness for purpose for understanding student learning in a mass higher education system (Haggis 2003), and its silence on the broader structural societal inequalities which set up barriers to learning (Ashwin and McLean 2004), there is no disputing the fact that the work put the learning experience of individual students firmly at the centre of considerations of teaching in higher education. The whole approach, in terms of both research and practice, was based on the presupposition that attention to a body of academic content was at the heart of both teaching and the learning of the subject. The primary concern was how students could be helped to make better sense of what they were learning in their courses of study.

By the mid-1990s technological developments were beginning to signal a new set of parameters for both curriculum design and course delivery, and new conversations were developing about how best to support student learning, taking the use of information and communication technologies into account. For example, Laurillard (1993) built on the phenomenographic tradition in developing her conversational model of learning, exploring in-depth how students engaged with academic knowledge, in contrast with their day-to-day understandings of the subject under study. Her work was clearly framed within a traditional view of the learner's engagement with disciplinary knowledge; she used examples from the natural sciences to support her argument that students and tutors were in a dialogue that was continually being refined, through both internalized conversations on the part of the learner and external feedback from the tutor. Although the focus was on an ongoing dialogue and reflection on learning, the teacher was seen as the expert and the student the novice. In particular, according to Laurillard, the role of the university teacher was to enable the student to engage with second-order, academic discourses, in contrast to first-order, everyday discourse about the subject under study. In a seminal volume, Laurillard built on this model in outlining a new agenda for university teaching with the advent of new technologies, emphasizing the possibilities for the collaborative nature of knowledge construction between students and tutors. In common with the work of Marton *et al.* (1984), she reinforced the critique of a 'transmission' model of learning. As new technologies began to be used more widely in the sector, not just for students studying at a distance but also for those in face-to-face institutions, new ways of thinking about learning and the learner began to dominate; nevertheless, disciplines and subjects were still at the heart of these approaches. Gradually, as technologies began to provide possibilities for students to learn together in meaningful ways, for example, through the use of discussion in computer conferencing, there was a shift away from attention to the independent (individual) learner to notions of collaborative learning (Thorpe 2002). Such approaches had already surfaced in higher education during the early 1990s, with an emphasis on group work, and even group assessment (Gibbs 1995), but with the advent of new technologies there was an increased focus on collaboration and interaction as ways of supporting student engagement in understanding the subject under study. The attempt to move away from what was seen at the time as an unfavourable transmission model of learning, based on behavioural theories and methods, was supported by Vygotskian principles of scaffolding, collaboration and understandings of situated learning (see Chapters 2 and 4 for further discussion).

Concurrent with these developments in approaches to student learning, others, too, were turning their attention towards a perceived shift in the status of the production of different kinds of knowledge, in and outside the university. In 1994, Gibbons and his colleagues first suggested a distinction between different forms of knowledge production (Gibbons *et al.* 1994). Whereas mode 1 knowledge was based on traditional research in established academic disciplines, mode 2 knowledge production was interdisciplinary and problem-focused. This categorization distinguished between disciplinary knowledge produced by, and legitimated by, disciplinary communities in academic settings and institutions, and knowledge produced in work-based and everyday contexts outside of the university. Because mode 2 knowledge is detached from educational institutions, it is primarily produced and valorized for its utility in the 'context of application' (Usher 2000: 232). Barnett (1997) makes similar distinctions in highlighting the performative and experiential basis of legitimate knowledge produced in workplace contexts, which contrasts with the more theoretical and disciplinary-based knowledge of the university. Students learning online through collaborative activity and discussion are often encouraged to engage in mode 2 knowledge production, for example, as professionals working together in postgraduate online courses. Such approaches are taken up enthusiastically and espoused by learning technologists. However, the success of online collaborative learning has yet to be fully proven as a model for learning in more conventional disciplinary-based undergraduate courses, and indeed it seems likely that social networking sites, such as Facebook, will be more likely to appeal to undergraduates than online computer conferencing and discussion boards (see Chapters 3 and 6 for further discussion). In contrast to approaches to learning which foreground the learner in relation to more established bodies of disciplinary knowledge, a shift towards mode 2 knowledge production challenges our preconceptions about what counts in the different curricula of the university and their relationship to work-based knowledge outside higher education.

Language and knowing: learning and writing

A further development in understanding student learning, driven initially by research in the USA, has seen the spotlight turned towards the complex relationship between learning and the writing of disciplinary knowledge. Nearly 20 years ago, a seminal work by Charles Bazerman identified how disciplinary difference was manifest in the writing practices of disciplinary experts, providing evidence for the ways in which disciplines were constructed through written texts with their own specific disciplinary norms and conventions (Bazerman 1988). Outlining how academic texts serve to construct subject knowledge in particular ways, he examined three published texts from established academics in molecular biology, literary criticism and sociology, in relation to four particular textual features: the object under study; the literature of the field; the anticipated audience; and the author's own self. His detailed analysis indicated how 'in mediating reality, literature, audience and self, each text seems to be making a different kind of move in a different kind of game' (Bazerman 1988: 46). In essence, the writer does not merely reflect the discipline, but the very act of writing continues the project of codifying the discipline in distinct ways:

> Getting the words right is more than a fine tuning of grace and clarity; it is defining the entire enterprise. And getting the words right depends not just on an individual's choice. The words are shaped by the discipline – in its communally developed linguistic resources and expectations; in its stylized identification and structuring of realities to be discussed; in

its literature; in its active procedures of reading, evaluating and using texts; in its structured interactions between writer and reader. The words arise out of the activity, procedures, and relationships within the community.

(Bazerman 1988: 47)

Berkenkotter and Huckin (1995) built further on this perspective in their concern with the nature of the discursive and communicative practices of academic writers in specific disciplinary contexts. They focused upon the analysis of written genres, suggesting that these genres form part of a discipline's methodology since they 'package information that conforms to a discipline's norms, values and ideology' (Berkenkotter and Huckin 1995: 1). These debates around the nature of disciplinary knowledge and its central relationship to writing the discipline and issues of epistemology coincided with increased attention, at first in the USA, to the difficulties that students experienced in their engagement with academic discourse in the learning process: 'The student has to learn to speak our language, to speak as we do, to try on peculiar ways of knowing, selecting, evaluation, reporting, concluding and arguing that define the discourse of our community'. (Bartholomae 1986: 134).

A long-established tradition of freshman composition, accompanying widening access to mass education, fuelled the US college composition movement, where much of the early work on student writing and its relationship to learning was carried out (Shaughnessy 1977; Flower and Hayes 1981; Bizzell 1982; Bartholomae 1986). Simultaneously, in Australia, Ballard and Clanchy (1988), who adopted an anthropological approach to student writing, foregrounded the relationship between language and culture as a way of understanding more about literacy. By the early 1990s similar attention was beginning to be paid to student writing in higher education (Lea 1994; Thesen 1994; Lillis 1997; Ivanič 1998), driven in part by a disquiet concerning the limitations of the phenomenographic work to adequately theorize the contextual and institutional nature of learning (Lea and Street 1998). Authors argued that theoretical approaches from social anthropology and applied linguistics – with their focus on the contextual and social nature of language and literacies – offered perspectives which were able to take account of the multiple discourses and literacies which were involved in student learning in higher education. Focusing on the gaps between tutor and student expectations and understanding of assignment writing, research in this field offered more contested explanations of meaning-making than had been present in the field of student learning until that time. More recently these approaches have been taken up by researchers in the field of writing and online learning (Lea 2000, 2001; McKenna 2003; Goodfellow *et al.* 2004; Coffin and Hewings 2005; Goodfellow 2005b; Goodfellow and Lea 2005). In tandem with these developments, some practitioners have turned their attention towards the Writing in the Disciplines programmes, which are well-established in a number of US universities. For example, the Thinking

Writing Programme at Queen Mary, London (see Mitchell 2006) is strongly influenced by the work of Monroe (2002) who has examined the deep association between disciplinary writing and learning, arguing that, for a student, learning to write in an academic context can never be usefully separated from the epistemological concerns of the discipline; put another way, writing to learn and learning to write – an adaptation of James Britton's (1970) famous adage – are two sides of the same coin.

Research and practice in student writing have raised fundamental questions, not only with respect to how best to support student writers, but also with regard to the part that writing and reading play in the whole process of meaning-making in teaching and learning at university. The literacies perspective that we develop in this book takes, as its starting point, the position that writing is integrally linked to issues of epistemology in higher education whatever the technologies involved. The theoretical perspectives that guide this work are drawn from broader studies of language and literacies (Street 1984; Barton 1994; Gee 1996), and focus on social and contextual approaches to literacies in the university. These provide a valuable framing for exploring the relationships of power and authority in the process of learning and assessment, including what counts as knowledge in any particular contexts and how certain texts and practices become privileged (see Chapter 4 for a fuller discussion of academic literacies in particular). This nexus of research is important because in later chapters we argue that despite, or maybe because of, technological developments in e-learning, written text is predominating in student learning environments, although the nature of these texts may be undergoing fundamental changes, for example, in terms of their ease and speed of access and the possibilities for seamlessly merging documents (see Chapters 4 and 6 for further discussion).

Conclusion

This chapter has focused upon explorations of e-learning and its relationship to ongoing changes in higher education. I began by arguing that social and cultural theories of language and discourse provide a useful background in any examination of present-day policy towards e-learning, and drew on this in consideration of various official websites concerned with learning and technologies. In taking a lens to the language of web pages and policy statements and documents around learning, I have begun to unpack the part that e-learning is playing in the reconfiguration of higher education, in particular its role in the shifting of focus from learning through engagement in disciplinary bodies of knowledge towards the management of learning. This is juxtaposed with approaches to student learning which have been primarily concerned with issues of epistemology and, more specifically, with the part that writing and written texts play in the construction of knowledge. This, then, serves as an introduction for discussions which will be raised in later chapters in which we argue that, rather than foregrounding the 'management of learning', e-learning agendas should be primarily concerned with supporting learning as a complex, contextualized, meaning-making, textual activity tied to student engagement with bodies and systems of knowledge, whether academic, professional or vocational. In this endeavour, later chapters consider the texts and practices which are involved in e-learning, developing a perspective which takes as its starting point a view of writing and reading – conceptualized in their broadest sense across modes – as contextualized social practices. We offer an alternative to a benign interpretation of the effect of technology on learning, and the opportunity to take an institutional perspective on both e-learning and its associated texts. We argue that taking this approach is necessary if we are to understand more fully both the relationship between learning and technologies and the texts and practices that emerge in their association. In the chapters which follow, we suggest that we need to recognize and effectively engage with the complex ways in which language, broader social and cultural contexts and technologies interact in online environments, and to foreground the social and linguistic practices involved in the use of electronic technologies in higher education. Our perspective, with its particular focus on texts and the process of meaning-making, offers an examination of the social and cultural practices implicated in any learning context and which, we believe, established e-learning pedagogies have so far failed to address.

2

Learning technologies in the university: from 'tools for learning' to 'sites of practice'

Robin Goodfellow

In Chapter 1, Mary set out the case for regarding the discourses of e-learning as a 'dominant paradigm' for teaching and learning in the university. She argued that the current heavy promotion of new technologies in higher education reflects national educational policies and commercial strategy at an organizational level, but is only marginally related to thinking about student learning or teaching in the disciplines. The case for our challenging the growing influence that this agenda is exercising over higher education practice does not rest on any objection in principle to the use of technologies in teaching, nor on a neo-luddite resistance to change in the conditions of teaching and learning we ourselves are experiencing. We accept that much e-learning practice is of benefit to students in enhancing the quality and flexibility of their learning. We also acknowledge that e-learning is, in one sense, unchallengeable, as it is a manifestation in the university context of much wider social and technological changes that are affecting all sectors of Western society in the globalized conditions of our times. Our wish to problematize its growing influence in higher education, derives from concern about a widening gap between the natural aspiration of subject-based teachers that academic content should be at the heart of teaching and learning, and the focus of institutions on managing learning through systems and processes, rather than supporting learners in their engagement with disciplinary and subject-based knowledge. In making this challenge we are looking to bridge this gap, by bringing the discourses of new technology and of teaching and learning together within a single frame of reference, that of the literacy practices which define the business of 'doing university work', whether on campus or at a distance, as a student, teacher, researcher, manager or technician, working in established disciplinary, or newly interdisciplinary, professional or occupational fields. In doing so we hope to persuade today's enthusiastic e-learning practitioners to view themselves not simply as pedagogical innovators, but as inheritors of epistemological value systems that are very deep-rooted in Western societies. Similarly, we wish to encourage discipline-based academics to see the increasing technologization of their practice not only as an administrative threat or occasional convenience, but as part of a newly-emerging communicative order which has the potential to link them and their students into widening, and increasingly eclectic, knowledge-generating networks.

In this chapter and the next, I will discuss what I see as a shift that needs to come about in the way the relation between new technologies and learning is conceptualized, if the dominant institutional construction of e-learning as the solution to the problems of reconfiguring higher education is to be successfully challenged. This shift is away from the metaphor of the computer as a 'tool' for learning, a legacy from earlier generations of computer-based learning (CBL) which still underpins much current e-learning pedagogy, and towards the notion of the technology as a 'site' of social practice. The tool-for-learning metaphor is implicit in the response of the JISC to the then Department for Education and Science questionnaire on e-learning that was referred to in the previous chapter: that the value of e-learning is wholly dependent on the purpose for which it is applied. This is a simple extension of the common-sense notion of the computer as a tool that can be applied to a range of tasks, such as word-processing, number-crunching, image generation, etc. The metaphor decouples the technology from its actual context of use and puts the outcome into the hands of the user. Pedagogical approaches built on this metaphor tend to foreground the individual learner's knowledge and skills in the use of the tool, which appeals on an intuitive level because ICT skills are socially valued and increasingly central to many aspects of contemporary life. The term 'knowledge worker', now in common use, serves precisely to underline the economic significance of these skills. At a deeper level the tool-for-learning metaphor draws on a tradition of thinking about human learning that derives from cognitive psychology, and particularly from the association of learning with memory. The idea of the computer as a tool for leveraging human cognitive performance, enabling us to calculate faster, recall more efficiently, select and match more accurately, fits easily with a view of learning as the development of an individual's information processing capabilities (see Crook 1994: 51–4, for a very informative discussion on the contribution of the information processing metaphor to educational thinking).

However, the tool metaphor marginalizes other, equally important, dimensions of learning with technologies that are always present – such as the social identities of participants, the cultures of institutions, the modes of communication and the practices of communities. These dimensions have a crucial role to play in the transformation of the students' learning experience too, but they are often much less 'visible' or executable than the technical systems which can be put into the hands of learners and teachers and observed in operation. Thinking of technologies not as tools but as 'sites' where various kinds of social practices are played out – a conceptualization inspired by Street's (1995: 162) view of literacy as a 'site of tension' between authority and individual creativity – means paying attention to these more general and pre-existing social relations, while being aware of how technical systems inflect them and are inflected by them, for everyone involved in their institutional use, not just the individual user as learner. From this perspective, e-learning is one part of the context in which we develop our practice as teachers and learners in the university, a role that it shares with other aspects of the environment, such as the people we interact with, the other materials and technologies we employ and, most importantly, the values and practices of the other institutions and organizations whose interests and activities border on, and overlap with, those of the university.

The notion of 'practice' is of some importance in the argument we are developing throughout this book, so I will take a moment to explain how I am using it in this chapter and the next. It is one of those words which carries a large repertoire of common-sense associations but is nevertheless very difficult to define. In discussions about learning, apart from its everyday meaning in the sense of 'rehearse', and the (in my view) somewhat facile deployment of the expression 'best practice' as a synonym for 'what works', it is very often linked to occupational contexts, as it is in Schön's (1991) work on the reflective practice of professional learners or that of Lave and Wenger (1991; Wenger 1998) on communities of practice. For the purposes of this discussion I am using 'practice' in both a general and a specific sense. The general sense draws on Pierre Bourdieu's (1977) notion of the usual pattern of how things are done or happen in given cultural contexts. Bourdieu used the statistical regularity of the occurrence of certain behaviours as a means to identify the more ritualistic patterns of social interaction in the societies he studied, such as behaviours around marriage, or gift exchanging occasions. But he extrapolated the idea of socially recognized regularity in behaviour to other informal and less clearly describable ways of proceeding: ways of talking, moving, making things, the manner in which actors 'carry themselves', etc. (Jenkins 1992: 75). The recognizable regularities in these behaviours and interactions are accounted for by culturally given dispositions and interests which incorporate both agency – people choosing what they do from moment to moment – and social structure – expectations that 'cause' people to do certain things at certain times (Bourdieu refutes the idea of scientific causality as a sufficient explanation of social behaviour). Practice in the domain of teaching and learning describes the things that people do, and the way they are, when they are recognizably acting as teachers and learners, and the strategic goals that consciously or unconsciously motivate them to act in this way. It also incorporates the locations or sites where this enactment of roles and goals typically goes on: in offices, classrooms and lecture halls, campuses and homes, on computer desktops and in virtual sites across the Internet.

In the more specific sense in which I use the term 'practice', I am drawing on the concept of 'literacy practice' in educational settings (Street 1995; see also Chapter 4): the written and oral conventions of language use that occur in the specific social contexts of teaching and learning in the university, for example, the things we do in a seminar – take notes, read from texts, borrow from a variety of written and spoken genres. The notion of literacy practice attaches great importance to the meanings and values attributed to specific instances of textual communication by participants, such as the sending and receiving of an email. These contextualized values – who has the right to message whom at this moment, what language should be used, who should be copied in – construct the email as social action as well as communication, having implications for relations (including relations of power) between the participants. Contextualized values attached to literacy practices can be contrasted with the view that there is some absolute set of social values that makes certain types of writing always better than others, like always writing 'proper sentences' or never making spelling mistakes. The concept of literacy practice also seeks to put into its social context emergent characteristics of textual communication that might otherwise be thought to result primarily from the technical mode of its production, for example, the short and ungrammatical sentences that Susan Herring and others attribute to the use of synchronous 'chat' media with its accelerated time-scales and rapidly scrolling canvas (Herring 2001). My use of the term 'practice' in this sense begins with the idea that people using technologies in learning contexts are engaged in activities that have particular social meanings derived from our recognition of them as 'ways of proceeding' in the particular social contexts in which they occur. For example, switching on my computer and logging on to read my emails has one set of social meanings, shared by my colleagues, if I do it in my office at 9 o'clock on a Monday morning in a working week, and another set of meanings if I do it from an Internet café in Kerala one afternoon during my annual holiday. When I come to considering the nature of our increasingly technologized learning practices in more detail, it will be in terms of background considerations like this, as well as the more overt kinds of meaning that are routinely attached to the different sorts of communication bundled up under the label of doing learning with technologies.

In what follows, I will look at some of the pedagogical approaches to CBL that form the basis of what we currently call e-learning, and particularly at the metaphor of the computer as a tool for learning, and the way that it has become translated into current practice. Metaphorical shifts in the discourses of teaching and learning are not single events, of course, and the tool-for-learning metaphor itself already represents a shift from an earlier, perhaps less intuitively acceptable, notion of the computer as tutor – a transmitter of knowledge in its own right, able to take the place of a human teacher, as characterized in some of the early designs of CBL and intelligent tutoring systems. Moreover, a further shift is already going on in the discourse around online learning communities, towards a more 'ecological' metaphor foregrounding the learning environment as a site for interaction (Young *et al.* 2000), which involves an explicit theoretical reorientation away from the individualistic, mentalistic, perspectives typical of CBL with its cognitive-psychological underpinnings. The ecological perspective leans towards more social and anthropological framings, such as those that inform thinking about learning in 'situated', 'community', and 'networked' learning contexts (Brown *et al.* 1989; Lave and Wenger 1991; Barab and Duffy 2000). However, at the same time as pedagogical practice in formal educational contexts is embracing the principle of learning as participation (see Sfard's 1998 account of this as a metaphor in its own right), learners themselves are raising issues concerning the amount of time that full participation requires and the restricted flexibility for independent study that ecological approaches imply (see the discussion under 'Sites for interaction' below). A strong market for independent learning has developed in the informal sector (corporate training, hobbyist study, other lifelong learning contexts) which has produced a conceptual shift in the opposite direction, back towards the idea of the decontextualized 'learning object' which allows the learner to construct their own meaning, independently of any overt teaching or collaborative effort. In the concept of learning design, which is discussed later, we can even detect a return to elements of the original computer-as-tutor metaphor, with corresponding implications for the role of teachers themselves and their status within the disciplinary communities they inhabit.

The argument for a metaphorical shift, therefore, is not about adopting particular kinds of pedagogical approach, although we will be examining specific examples of pedagogical practice in our case studies later in Chapter 5. Rather, it is an attempt to locate the concept of e-learning practice within a more comprehensive context of teaching and learning than is provided by current discourses. As we will argue throughout the book, it is the social practices of the university itself, as embedded in its linguistic communication, that do most to determine the nature of the student learning experience, whether the learning environment be electronic, print-based or face-to-face.

Tools for learning

Of all the modern devices that have been adapted for educational use (telephone, radio, film camera, TV, tape recorder, video recorder, etc.), the personal computer has probably had the greatest impact. Not only has it taken over most of the functions that used to be performed by a range of other devices (writing, calculating, designing, storing, organizing, etc.), it has come to be regarded as a kind of mental prosthetic, a way of extending human information processing capacity beyond what the unaided brain is capable of. Today, in its networked mode, the computer is also seen as a practically limitless source of information, and as a point of access to knowledge construction activity in an almost limitless number of domains. The acquisition of the skills involved in using computers is now seen as of equal priority for learning as the development of habits of print-based reading and writing, with the UK Quality Assurance Agency's (QAA) review of subject teaching in universities in 2001 reporting that 'Competence in the use of information and communication technology ... was generally seen as a key transferable skill', and that 'all institutions and subjects treated the development of students' ICT skills as a key objective' (QAA 2001a: 15).

It was not so in the early days of CBL, and in fact the rise of the computer as a tool for learning has not been quite as meteoric as is often implied, having taken about a quarter of a century (a generation) to come to its current prominence. One reason for this might be that a long time was spent working through the earlier metaphor of computer as tutor, in search of designs that would substitute for human tutors in the delivery of instruction. The very earliest attempts to do this were based on simple branching algorithms that could be used to direct the presentation of new material in response to the learner's performance. For example, a correct answer would take you along one path through the material, a partially correct one would direct you along another and an incorrect one might hold you where you were until you got it right. As Crook (1994: 13–4) has observed, systems that operated on this principle continued to be used quite widely for early years schooling, but they did not meet with the same success where learners were more demanding or the domains of study more complex. The search for a more sophisticated computer tutor was taken up in the 1980s by researchers in the field of artificial intelligence, many of whom had long been attracted by the notion of a synergy between computation and human thought. Computer processing provides a compelling model of human thinking, if the latter is conceived of as the flow, storage and retrieval of symbols, and their conversion into representations (see Anderson 1996 for a highly developed operational model of human information processing along these lines). Computer programming languages, such as LISP and Prolog, which were designed to represent logical relations between facts, rather than simply performing operations on numbers, themselves introduced a powerful new idea for thinking about thinking, giving rise to a branch of psychology known as cognitive science which set out to produce feasible models of human problem-solving. The processing that these models carried out was thought to mimic human higher reasoning processes, conjuring the idea that machines could eventually come to 'know' things in a manner analogous to human experts. The field of CBL was inspired by this analogy, and intelligent tutoring systems were designed and developed to test new theories about how knowledge, in various domains, could best be represented for transmission to the minds of learners (see Wenger 1987 for an overview). Few of these systems made the transition from prototype to classroom practice, however, for a variety of reasons, not least of which was the very limited domains in which they could operate. One of the more intractable complexities of real human thinking, from the point of view of knowledge-based systems design, is the way it draws on multiple and sometimes analogous sources to solve problems, not simply the rules and precedents of the problem domain itself.

One of the pioneers whose work did most to move the field on from computers as tutors, away from drill-and-practice programs and the behaviourist psychology on which they were based, and away from the cul-de-sac of the intelligent tutoring system, was Seymour Papert (1980). Papert, who can probably be regarded as the father of the metaphor of the computer as a tool for learning, developed an approach to teaching children maths based on the exploration of a mathematical 'microworld' consisting of a robot device, called a 'turtle', controlled by a simplified computer program called Logo. Children could use Logo to enter instructions into the computer and this would make the turtle move around and describe geometrical shapes. Papert proposed that to make the conscious connection between the instructions given to the computer, and the physical shapes of the turtle's movement, was to experience a 'powerful idea' which once learned would itself become a building block for more and more complex conceptual structures. Such ideas he referred to as 'tools for thinking', a metaphor framed by the constructivist paradigm that many cognitive and developmental psychologists were working within at the time (Bruner *et al.* 1956; Ausubel 1968; Piaget 1972). Constructivism is an account of the way that representations of the world are built up in the minds of human beings in the form of schemas and mental models that relate new information to what has already been learned. The process provides the basis for the formation of abstract concepts, and Papert argued that practical activity – the physical control of the turtle's movements – can serve as a reliable basis for building abstract schemas, such as those related to the use of formal description languages like Logo and mathematical notation. He did not believe in the computer as tutor, intelligent or otherwise. In his view the technology merely helped children to construct understandings for themselves.

Papert established a new role for the digital computer as a tool capable of stimulating constructive mental activity leading to learning. But there were critics who pointed out that to attribute this mental activity solely to the learner's interaction with the computer and turtle system was to ignore the influence of any teaching that might be going on in parallel (Crook 1994: 28). Others argued that the very close affinity between the tool and the knowledge domain in this case – there is an exact correspondence between the numbers typed into the computer and the degree to which the turtle moves in response – means that the learner does not need to develop any actual understanding of Logo at all (Laurillard 1993: 143). Direct manipulation of a system in order to solve a problem bypasses the need for an explicit language of description and representation, which some consider to be the real object of academic learning. Laurillard argues that the intuitive knowledge of the physical world that is gained by 'playing' with Papert's turtles may be useful to the learner but will not necessarily help them to articulate the rules underlying the relationship between the symbols on the screen and the movement of the turtle. In this view, academic learning, as a distinct way of experiencing the world via a language of description, requires the progressive adaptation of the learner's conceptualization of the domain in collaborative conversation with an expert (teacher's) viewpoint. The computer functions as a tool for constructive learning, therefore, not only by affording the learner an opportunity to experiment with the manipulation of a system, but also by supporting the progressive exchange of viewpoints between learner and teacher/expert on the results of the manipulation. In order to do this, the system is required to embed the teacher/expert's side of the dialogue into its responses.

In the pregraphical interface era of personal computers, before the windows, mouse and menus convention for user control of the computer that was first popularized by the Apple Mac in the mid-1980s, and which has since become the standard interface, the only way a computer could engage in a dialogue with its user was via written language. Human language being highly complex, the challenge of designing a computer that could 'talk' to its user has fascinated computer scientists for years, ever since Alan Turing (1950) first proposed that the ability to do this as well as a human interlocutor, would be evidence that the machine was thinking for itself. The goal has never been achieved, although it continues to fascinate wishful designers of 'intelligent' computer programs, as witnessed by the annual Loebner prize competition which subjects specially designed programs to a literal Turing test (the program attempts to convince judges that they are interacting with a human), with sometimes surreal results (transcripts from the 2005 Loebner prize for computer conversation can be found on the web at http://loebner.net/Prizef/2005_Contest/Transcripts.html, accessed February 2007). Linguistic dialogue, as a tool for learning, has proved too complex even to be simulated in the limited domains of CBL systems. The highly contextualized nature of language in use, drawing on a range of knowledge about conventions of interaction and histories of previous exchange as well as syntactic and semantic systems of disambiguation, ensures that even if it were possible to give the computer complete coverage of the language of the subject matter this would still not be sufficient for it to conduct a properly human-like dialogue. Language is, in fact, not simply another kind of interface through which communication is conducted, but is itself constitutive of communication in a very active way. It is this complex constructive role that both provokes our concern that there has been so little attention paid to language in the context of e-learning (see Chapter 4), and also partly explains it, as there is clearly a tradition in CBL of failing to come to terms with it!

The development of direct manipulation graphical interfaces, together with the increased processing power of a new generation of micro-computers supporting multiple media (colour graphics, audio, video, animation) and, most importantly, the innovation of hypertext, enabled the problem of learner–computer dialogue to be sidestepped, and gave the constructivist perspective a new focus in the learning that might be generated through the use of complex mediated environments for problem-solving. Jonassen *et al.* (1993) summarized this principle in a 'manifesto' for constructivist teaching in higher education, which laid claim to a specific relevance of this model of learning for the university context. According to the constructivist manifesto, universities are particularly concerned with the 'advanced knowledge acquisition' phase of learning, which occurs between the introductory and the expert stages. This phase is:

facilitated by environments that represent multiple realities, that use real-world, case-based contexts for learning, and facilitate collaborative construction of knowledge. These environments should be supported by tools that engage learners meaningfully. All of these activities can be effectively supported by technology-based environments.

(Jonassen *et al.* 1993: Section 6.0)

The manifesto argued that computer technologies enable learners to experience environments that reflect the informational complexities of the real world, and to engage with problems that are meaningful in this context. In this way they can be helped to generate their own knowledge base which is relevant to the external world, but which is personal, individualistic and can be shared and renegotiated with others. Learning, in this view, is a product of deep analysis that is facilitated by material that has been acted on or generated by the learners themselves. Both analytical and generative processes are supported by cognitive tools all of which are computational: semantic networking software, expert systems, databases and microworlds. Most notably, the dialogue with a teacher/expert is reconceptualized as a process of guided exploration, rather than actual conversation, with the learner following pathways, tasks and checks that the teacher/expert has embedded in the system itself. Learning via guided exploration through hypermedia environments presented both a stimulating challenge to constructivist instructional designers, and a potential solution to the economic strictures of increasing student numbers, as it appeared to offer a means by which university teachers could work with larger group sizes. The result was that a number of publicly funded development projects were launched during the 1990s (see Chapter 1), which were aimed primarily at supplementing or replacing existing teaching practice in selected university contexts with self-access and self-paced interaction with multimedia programs designed on constructivist principles.

A lot of hypermedia systems were built and piloted during this period (see the Liverpool University Chemistry Department's list of systems developed for this subject area alone at http://www.liv.ac.uk/ctichem/swalph.html), but, like the CBL and artificial intelligence systems that preceded them, few found their way into established teaching practice, and many went out of date or out of favour long before they had repaid their university's investment in terms of student use. The example of one particular system developed by the University of Cape Town (UCT) Multimedia Education Group (MEG – now the Centre for Educational Technology; see http://www.cet.uct.ac.za) illustrates well the problems that many multimedia initiatives faced in sustaining the constructivist pedagogical principle of guided self-exploration, and also in responding to changes in university policy or curriculum in the longer term. In 1997 the MEG began to work with the university Writing Centre to develop tutorials supporting students in developing an understanding of conventions of referencing and the use of information from external sources (Deacon *et al.* 1997). The aim of the project was to teach first-year students in English and history about the ways in which multiple sources are used in various disciplines, and why they should acknowledge the source of their information in essays. Explicitly constructivist elements of the design of the multimedia tutorials included the principle of orientation via a familiar metaphor, chunking of information, simple tasks followed by more complex ones, 'deep' processing facilitated by constructive activity, the use of graphics to engage those with a visual orientation (e.g. a visual metaphor equating the logical structure of an essay to the parts of a classical façade), and a variety of hypertext-based activities and tasks for exploration and reflection. In the trials of this system it was found that although students found the program motivating and there was improvement in the referencing practices of some students, many of them continued to approach the program by seeking a 'correct' linear path through the material, rather than by engaging in open exploration of the hypertextual environment, a reversion to a more conventional 'instructional' paradigm. This illustrates our point that teaching and learning practices are deeply imbricated with the established literacies of the institution – in this case the practice of 'reading' the material in the linear manner more suited to print, despite its digital and hypertextual nature. Despite the resources that went into the development of this system, and a positive evaluation of the pilot, it was used with UCT Humanities students for only one year, and with students at a neighbouring college for two more. One of the developers has noted that wider institutional factors were responsible for this (Marion Walton, personal communication, 4 January 2006). The tutorials were tightly integrated into courses that ceased to exist when the Humanities faculty moved to a programmes-based structure. The new structure rested on large foundation courses, compulsory for all students in the faculty, and the logistics of greatly increased student numbers in relation to the problems of access to faculty computer labs meant that the MEG unit could not continue to support students using the multimedia materials. Again, this illustrates the point that even though the pedagogical grounding for a technological innovation in teaching and learning might be theoretically sound, it is the larger structures of the institution that will often determine whether the new practices are successfully integrated.

A further reason for the decline of stand-alone multimedia systems was the dramatic proliferation, from the mid-1990s onwards, of the World Wide Web and the Internet, offering low-cost access to interactive hypermedia combined with two-way human-to-human communication, creating for the first time the real possibility of collaborative peer learning at a distance and on a large scale. These learning technologies resonated with larger public discourses of change, around the emergence of what has been called variously the 'networked society' or the 'knowledge economy' (Castells 1996). From being a tool for the construction of personal knowledge, the computer, or more precisely the online environment, began to be thought of as a site for interaction leading to the collaborative construction of shared meaning, a process that makes the social dimension of online learning explicit.

Sites for interaction

Collaboration is another concept that is difficult to define, as it can be set against related notions, such as co-operation and collegiality, which vary in degree of task orientation and level of required commitment (Burbules 2000). Nevertheless, collaborative learning has been the principal motivation behind much of the effort that has gone into the development of teaching approaches that use computer-mediated communication (CMC), and it remains a key strategy in the rhetoric and practice of e-learning. Online collaborative learning draws on a co-constructivist, or social-constructivist, rationale, common to the work of seminal thinkers in the field of child development, such as Dewey (1998) and Vygotsky (1978). Vygotskian socio-cultural theories about the role of the social in the development of mental states, and specifically the notion that social interaction precedes individual learning, have been particularly influential in the field of collaborative online learning, although generally without following up on the key role that Vygotsky assigned to language in the process (see Chapter 4 for further discussion). Socio-cultural theory become one of the 'innovations in learning theory' (King 1998: 370) on which early practitioners and researchers based their approach to online learning (Mason and Kaye 1989; Berge and Collins 1995; Bonk and King 1998b), focusing on the promotion of group work and other forms of peer-to-peer interaction intended to develop both the individual's thinking and their ability to scaffold the cognitive development of others. The enthusiasm of the early adopters of online collaborative learning, in the face of difficulties posed by the unreliable CMC technologies of the period, was motivated by more than a simple desire for technical or pedagogical innovation. For these pioneers of e-learning, online collaborative learning was, as Harasim (1989) pronounced, 'a unique domain', signifying the arrival of the communication age in the university. The accompanying discourses are thus not only about pedagogical effectiveness, but also about the transformation and democratization of higher education. The role of the computer as a site for group interaction was seen as to remedy constraints caused by class sizes, lack of available resources, student apathy, etc., and to extend the benefits of collaborative learning to remote and globally distributed participants, as well as to deliver individual and group cognitive development.

Although these discourses of collaborative learning work to position pedagogical and technological innovation as symbiotic, the rhetoric of 'powerful tools to break the traditional mold of education' (King 1998: 368) nevertheless, serves to celebrate the technologies principally because they are new and offer a challenge to conventional practice in the university. However, accounts of actual pedagogical practice in collaborative online learning seldom do justice to the oft-repeated claim that the impact of CMC is of a similar order to that of the invention of the printing press. Many describe a fairly basic level of debate that is no more than would be expected in a reasonably successful face-to-face classroom. Descriptions of innovative work, such as the account of US school-based learners accessing remote sites of authentic and often exciting real-world activity, that Sugar and Bonk (1997) provide in their discussion of a project called the World Forum, developed at the University of Michigan, are notable exceptions. Although the pioneers of online learning set out to make a case for an overall paradigm shift in the purpose and structure of education based on social-constructivist and collaborative learning principles, it is the technology rather than the educational mission that has subsequently emerged as the main impetus for practical change. In the spirit of Bonk and King's (1998a: xxv) observation that 'technological breakthroughs alter the way we learn, research, work and socialize', the development of new pedagogies of online learning almost inevitably comes to focus on finding ways to use the new tools effectively, rather than on implementing the transformation of learning explicit in the rhetoric. Thus collaborative learning, despite its long pre-computer pedagogical history (Dewey 1938), is now associated with a call for educational reform as a response to the demands of technologized conditions of knowledge production, a process Mary has described in the context of higher education as a whole in Chapter 1.

I would argue that while socio-cultural learning theory continues to provide the justification for much pedagogical practice in e-learning, its usefulness as an account of teaching and learning practice in online environments has diminished as the complexity of the technical and sociological dimensions has increased. As a theory, its subsequent refinements, including cultural historical activity theory (Engeström 1990), remain very productively at the heart of psychologically-oriented research into working and learning with technologies. In Chapter 5 we discuss a case study from an American university in which the pedagogical design is based on principles from activity theory, but in general I would suggest that the application of social-constructivist ideas to online educational practice has provided neither the insights into individuals' experience of learning, nor the remedies for lack of participation and failure to learn online, that might have been expected in the two decades or so that have passed since collaborative online learning was pioneered. In fact the original social-constructivist accounts of peer-to-peer collaborative knowledge construction as expressed in Bonk and King (1998b), referred to above, have now been supplanted by a broader range of theoretical and pragmatic positions focusing on the 'online learning community' as a site of educational interaction. Closest among these to the spirit of both Papert and the socio-cultural learning theorists are approaches from the research fields of computer supported collaborative learning, which continue to draw on both Vygotsky and the principle of 'designing' computer-based interactions as tools for learning. Ravenscroft (2005), for example, describes an attempt to ally a developmental model of online community to a theory of cognitive 'transformation' through structured educational dialogue. In this approach, the online environment is a tool with which the interaction of participants can be guided and shaped, so that it eventually produces a certain kind of structured discourse believed to facilitate learning. As with Papert's approach of 25 years earlier, the implication is that it does not need teaching intervention, but only interaction as designed, to bring about the transformation of the learner. Less prescriptive but still broadly psychologically-based are analyses of online learning communities which draw on the concept of 'social presence' to characterize learning through interaction. Social presence can be conceptualized as predominantly affective, as in accounts of the effect on learning of learners' experiences of a motivational 'sense of community' derived from interaction with remote peers (Rovai 2002). It can also be both affective and cognitive, as Garrison *et al.* (2001) propose in their discussion of 'teaching presence' – a necessary condition, alongside social presence, for maintaining the focus on which the community's collective learning is dependent. Perhaps furthest theoretically from socio-cultural learning theory are accounts which draw on social network theory, such as those of Haythornthwaite (2002) and other contributors to Renninger and Shumar's book *Building Virtual Learning Communities* (2002), who characterize online learning communities in terms of the 'ties', either weak or strong, that sociologists have shown are created among participants on the basis of the exchange of informational goods and services that are mutually valued (Wellman and Gulia 1999).

Rather more prominent in current practice contexts than any of these theoretical perspectives, however, is the more general perception of the online learning community as a site where social interaction fosters a learning process analogous to the socialization that goes on in communities which are physically located (Wallace 2003 provides a useful review of these approaches). In this view, if the conditions for the development of community are put in place online, then learning arises naturally and collectively (Paloff and Pratt 1999). Models that describe this process in terms of a progression of types of interaction, proceeding from technical contact to basic socialization to eventual collaboration and knowledge construction, have been applied to the organization of online learning on quite a large scale, for example, the UK National College for School Leadership's adoption of the 'community' metaphor and of Salmon's (2000) five-stage model of community interaction for the training of online moderators responsible for managing the learning of thousands of participants across the college's many training programmes (Carmichael *et al.* 2005). This view of interaction proposes developmental stages that participants go through in the course of building a community online. Typically, there is an initial technical stage in which individuals learn to access and use the conferencing system; an interim social stage in which online groups are formed and a 'sense of community' develops; and a culminating, knowledge constructing stage characterized by independent learning, critical and reflective thinking, and the renegotiation of participant roles (Salmon 2000). Virtual learning communities are thus conceived of as 'built' phenomena organized around explicit goals which may be imposed by design and facilitated by expert moderators. However, the history of non-educational CMC is also replete with examples of undesigned and unmoderated online groups developing spontaneously around shared interests, such as occupations and hobbies, cultural or sexual identities, civic or political issues, etc. (Smith and Kollock 1999). Elsewhere I have discussed the ideological nature of the 'turn to community' in online education, and the role that virtual community initiatives in the IT industry, commerce, business training and teacher development have played in its construction (Goodfellow 2005a). What these unstructured communities have in common is that they exist, either in a real or an imagined sense, before the interaction which develops online. As Crook (1994: 216) suggests, it is the community that produces the communication, not the other way round.

The popularization of the role of 'moderator', in place of teacher, in the context of online learning communities, reflects the extent to which process has taken over from product in the conceptualization of learning, underlying current approaches to e-learning influenced by social-constructivist ideas about the construction of knowledge. This is a similar kind of change in orientation to the development of knowledge or expertise that characterized Papert's earlier version of constructivist learning which, as we have seen, was the subject of criticism by Laurillard and others for whom teaching was a crucial element missing from the story. Online learning communities thus represent a halfway point in the shift from the metaphor of the computer as a tool for learning to that of the site of practice. They are the current face of a continuing project to transform educational practice in line with new models of socialization defined by online communication (see the discussion on social media in Chapter 3). In the 'site of interaction' stage of the metaphorical shift, the individualism and mentalism of the Papert-era approach have given way to a focus on collaboration and social presence, with an underlying conceptualization of learning as an aided progression along a prescribed trajectory towards the 'centre' of the community, manifested either as expertise or as full engagement in core practices. However, the metaphor continues to foster the notion of the technology as a kind of leveraging device, capable by virtue of its design of adding value to the learner's attempts to acquire competence or status, 'levering novices into confidence', as Crook (2005) puts it. Moreover, process models of online interaction help to perpetuate the image of virtual environments as locations with the stability and permanence of a physical place, and as socially and culturally sealed off from the situated lives of their participants. This reflects the wider sense in which e-learning is couched in terms of the management of learning activity, rather than of teaching, helping to fulfil key policy aims of institutions committed to the technologization of their educational practice. The relative novelty of online collaborative learning, the support it receives from contemporary learning theory and its centrality to e-learning policy and strategy at governmental levels, have worked to construct the celebratory rhetoric we have referred to and to ensure that accounts that are overtly critical of learning as participation in online communities, or which chronicle learner problems and dissatisfactions, are relatively rare in the e-learning literature. This is partly because the authors of informed accounts are often reporting on their own work and have a vested interest in presenting this as largely successful. It is also a function of the way that e-learning has become ideologically dominant in approaches to innovation in higher education, so that there is a predisposition to see it as benign. However, there is evidence of tension arising between the aim of practitioners of online educational interaction to transform student learning, including the values shaping relations between learners and moderator/teachers, and the tendency of universities to reinforce established institutional values in practice, whatever their political or strategic rhetoric.

For example, collaborative learning is difficult to connect to conventional assessment and accreditation procedures, and this is exacerbated online where 'evidence' of contribution to group work is necessarily limited, as even the constructivist manifesto authors noted (Jonassen *et al.* 1993: Section 5.3). The practice of compelling participation in online interaction by making it compulsory does not resolve this difficulty, as issues of student motivation and the judgement of quality of online contributions still remain (Goodfellow 2001). A variety of factors impact on online participation patterns in online university courses. Participation is influenced by access issues, individual experience, expectations and preferences, cultures and power discourses both inside and outside the online learning space (Beaudoin 2002; Oliver and Shaw 2003; Goodfellow and Hewling 2005). There is a consensus among practitioners that it is not easy to get a majority of students contributing to debates in computer conferences at any level, and that this may be due to any number of reasons: intimidation caused by the permanence of written contributions, fear of criticism or of looking stupid, reluctance to criticize for fear of being impolite, feeling lost or too far behind the discussion, not having mastered the medium or specialist language or simply being a 'freeloader'. Furthermore, the supposed benefits of online collaborative discussion are not obvious to many learners, and there is little evidence to contradict the fact that some do just as well in their assessment tasks without participating in an online community. For those whose dispositions or circumstances incline them to peripheral social engagement as part of their study, the obligation to participate in online interaction is rather less likely to result in an enhanced learning experience. Some learners in such contexts can be expected to experience difficulties that will never be properly resolved as long as participation remains compulsory. These difficulties might stem from a variety of tensions that are directly attributable to the conditions of remote participation in virtual educational environments: discomfort in disembodied encounters, for example, or inability to 'read' conditions of socialization off the exchanged texts, such as whether it is permissable to contradict or argue with the views of others; frustration with perceived non-participation of others; stress arising from the attempt to engage in all aspects of many-to-many interaction; alienation arising from the way that textual interaction norms are determined; disorientation caused by the behaviour of teacher/moderators or the invisibility of institutional processes. All these conditions combine disorienting and demotivating factors that may be due to institutional as well as technical and pedagogical practices.

In addition to mounting evidence that interaction in online learning communities does not necessarily transform institutional practice *per se*, and that learners may actively resist engagement in building them, the metaphor of the site for collaborative interaction is currently being challenged from a perspective which emphasizes the needs of individual learners for efficient, personalized, just-in-time 'solutions' to their lifelong learning needs (Wiley 2002). From this point of view, economic and commercial pressures drive the development of e-learning, rather than educational reform or new learning theory, and the niche marketing strategies that characterize large-scale Internet commerce are reproduced in the curriculum thinking of newly business-conscious institutions of higher education. Personalized online learning conflicts with the more organizationally focused visions of collaborative networks and virtual learning communities. Wiley (2002) has described it as a 'coming collision' between collaborative and individualized learning designs, a conflict which can also be seen as a confrontation between the interests of academics as teachers, and those who are seeking to standardize the design of online learning materials so as to 'enshrine' teaching in permanent form, reduce the costs of large-scale teaching and shift the control of curriculum to the learner as customer. Oliver (2005) associates this approach with what he calls the 'meta-data community' – referring to the technical-pedagogical practice of labelling digital teaching material with 'tags' that enable it to be classified and deployed automatically as part of a database of such material. Such an approach supposedly enables the learner to access highly modularized 'learning objects' from a variety of providers in order to make up their own customized course, maximizing flexibility for institutions and individuals and sharing the responsibility for successful learning between the learner and the system. This apparently radical e-learning strategy is in line with governmental policy, at least in the UK, as Oliver (2005: 74) shows with quotations from the 1997 Dearing Report. Personalized learning offers a more flexible framework than does the learning community model, if only because it removes the emphasis on participation in many-to-many interaction that has proved problematic for so many online course designs. However, its dependence on individual self-motivation and the 'fit' between the pre-specified design of learning objects and their incorporation into a learner-specified syllabus implies a high degree of autonomy on the part of the learner, especially in the absence of any allowance in the learning materials for the specific context of practice to which the learner is trying to relate. It is an important consideration whether learners who are not already familiar with the domains and processes of university study would be in a position to take advantage of the opportunity to personalize the learning context, in the absence of traditional student support structures (teachers, technical support, schedules) afforded by university study proper. This is particularly pertinent where students come from groups whose participation in higher education has been traditionally underrepresented, which includes some newly professionalized occupational areas (nursing, business) as well as those recently targeted by governments for widening, for example, first-generation entrants to university and ethnic minority students. Personalized learning for these constituencies is more likely to be closely identified with classroom-based or workplace-based learning, and the case for regarding the learning technologies they use as sites in which this practice is actualized, rather than as tools for their personal cognitive development or collective knowledge construction, is at its most pressing.

Although the overall approach to the personalization of learning is not based on learning theory in the same way that interaction-oriented pedagogical design has been, some developments have attempted to incorporate the benefits of theory-based pedagogy by 'designing in' teaching styles and learner models, much as an earlier generation of intelligent tutoring systems attempted to do. A development that has envisaged a convergence of this and the learning community approach is the Learning Design specification developed at the Open University of the Netherlands (OUNL). The Learning Design framework aims to supply the technical facilities that would enable distributed learners who have a common goal to interact in such a way as to create personal networks with the emergent properties of a learning community (e.g. sharing knowledge and providing mutual support). The context for this interaction is a set of learning activities which are designed on the basis of pedagogical principles derived from constructivist analyses of the conditions for learning, for example, the relation of new knowledge to prior knowledge in conditions of real-world problem-solving. In this idealization, lifelong learners (who are sometime learners and sometimes teachers), resource providers and software agents, interact interchangeably in the construction of both syllabus and learning community. Koper (2005) for example, gives an account of a Learning Design project at the OUNL's Centre for Expertise in Educational Technology in which participants used a software environment implementing Learning Design principles based on a knowledge management environment to help develop their expertise in the field of e-learning design. In this project a whole set of 'requirements for lifelong learning' were tested. These included:

> evolving facilities for the members to improve and share their expertise and build the competencies needed in a disciplinary field . . . govern [ment] by community policies that reflect the common goals and values of the membership . . . learning designs [that] are based on pedagogical models that are suitable for the discipline, the membership and the learning objectives (e.g. problem-based and learner-centred, formative assessment, knowledge and community-centred).
>
> (Koper 2005: 11)

In his evaluation of this project, Koper observes that learning did take place via the intensive discussions that occurred among participants, with materials produced and commented on, expertise developed and shared, and individual skills enhanced. However, given the fact that the participants were already involved in the centre's physical community of practice, it is necessary to be cautious about associating these learning outcomes with the notion of emergent social organization enabled by the technologies. The evaluation also flagged other issues critical to the idea of a lifelong learning network as a social rather than technological construct, such as the fact that some participants reported feeling that control was not distributed (as it was designed to be) because those who created activities for others to do kept a privileged level of ownership over the areas in which the activities took place. Participants also commented on the vulnerability of the overall process to fluctuations in individual participation, and the failure of community policies (such as an agreed reward system) to emerge. Evidently, the realization of self-organization by human actors within the designed environment was problematic – not only did they intuitively not do what the system was designed to enable them to do, but also some experienced stress and frustration in the process of trying, just as participants do in less structured and principled online learning environments.

The Learning Design approach is still in its infancy, as Weller explains, and is still predominantly an interesting research area rather than an established approach to e-learning (Weller 2007: Chapter 8). But it is, nevertheless, already informing the development of tools being incorporated into (VLE) systems in widespread use in higher education. The emergent community principle is also being adapted by the UK Open University to the development of its 'open content' database of learning materials offered free of charge on the Internet (http://openlearn.open.ac.uk), further discussed in Chapter 6. However, the Learning Design approach, despite its apparent focus on interaction, is concerned with the production of designs for learning that are independent of subject matter or of the teaching materials. This means it has little to say about the relation between learning and its social context, especially, as Oliver (2005: 76) points out, where that context is one of professional expertise that has a high tacit component which makes it difficult to articulate. As such I would argue that it is actually a direct heir to the tools-for-learning metaphor in its earlier precollaborative learning form.

Sites of practice

The shift of metaphor for learning technology, from tool for learning to site of interaction, brings us part of the way towards the focus on practice that I am arguing for here, and which we have set out to associate with an academic literacies approach to e-learning in this book. The implications of the shift include a change in some aspects of relations among teachers and learners, which is what we are seeing in the development of VLEs and collaborative learning practices, such as e-moderating and peer-to-peer teaching, but in other respects practices that have been established in universities for a long time continue to hold sway. Some of these practices are pedagogical in character, such as giving students assignments to do, but others are institutional, such as the awarding of credit on the basis of individual assessment, cultural, such as holding guest lectures and seminars, disciplinary, such as conducting experiments or field trips, or generically academic, such as using libraries or research databases. Many of these practices are subject to reshaping by the introduction of information and communication technologies, but similarly, the way that the technologies themselves are being redesigned for university use is shaped by educational practice. From the start, when the World Wide Web was just beginning to penetrate into academic practice, educational adopters were among the first to voice concern at the unstructured and hard-to-validate nature of its information resources, and the indiscriminate publishing that it encouraged. The result was the development of electronic learning resource banks, academic publication databases, corporate library subscription services, and a range of intranet-based support functions that construct the university as an interface between its 'members' and the chaotic public web. The design of electronic discussion spaces, too, has been influenced by educational requirements for certain kinds of groups (classes), types of discussion and monitoring of users (see Chapters 3 and 4 for further discussion of this). Most recently, the educational policy-led promotion of systems to support personal and professional development is shaping the redesign for e-portfolio use of technologies invented to enable social networking and electronic commerce; some examples of this are discussed in Chapter 6.

The incorporation of learning technologies into these wider arenas of university practice constructs the technologies themselves as sites of this practice. However, it is wrong to assume that in doing so, the underlying practices themselves are necessarily changed, and in the cases where the technology comes equipped with cultural expectations from some other domain, such as the association virtual communities have with the 'electronic homesteading' metaphor created by Rheingold (1993) and other pioneers, there can be conflicts between the expectations of users and the reality of use. This is, in my view, part of the explanation of the problems of extent and nature of participation that have arisen in so many online courses. An illustration from Crook (2002) summarizes it neatly. In his account of the attempt by one UK university to introduce the use of electronic discussion boards into student study practices, in order to encourage peer support conducted through informal online group conversation, he shows how, in practice, students made little use of it, preferring to use email or instant messaging simply to maintain contact as they moved about the campus. At the time of the study, in the late 1990s, electronic many-to-many discussion was still predominantly associated with use by interest groups who were dispersed in time and space. For these colocated students, email was a better cultural 'fit' with their actual study practices.

A further example of a clash between existing practice and expectations built into the design of technology is provided by Barab *et al.* (2001), who set out to create a virtual equivalent of the practice of observing teachers at work in the classroom. This was to be done through the online discussion of video samples of teachers at work, supported by group collaboration on the design and preparation of lesson plans, posting of questions about teaching and virtual workrooms. They also established three levels of membership (observer, active community member and contributing member), and created the roles of leader, critical friend and reviewer, for community members to take on in order to provide leadership in discussion. Despite this principled approach, Barab *et al.* observe that, over a period of a year, it failed to generate anything like a real community of teacher-users. Many teachers did not feel encouraged to participate, could not develop social relationships, and felt uncomfortable with the basic idea of criticizing other teachers' practice. Furthermore, tensions emerged over the sharing of 'everyday' as opposed to 'expert' practice. These came to light in argument over the content of some of the videos, which appeared to show 'bad science' being taught, even though the focus was supposedly on the approach to teaching and not on the subject knowledge *per se*. Despite the inventive design, the authors believed that the culture of teachers sharing pedagogical practice was simply not sufficiently well established. The requirements of community were not satisfied by simply providing instances of exemplary classroom practice, but demanded opportunities to share, reflect on and discuss actual practice, and, crucially, for the community to own itself and develop its own directions. Barab *et al.* point out that their most active contributors were those who already had a structured commitment, for example, in preservice teacher classes or projects. In order to build trust among the other participants, they suggested there was a need for face-to-face contact, and the development of other non-virtual means (including financial) to support teachers in their participation.

Conclusion

In 1986, Winograd, a computer scientist who originally made his name building artificially intelligent language-using systems, co-authored and published a book that set the scene for the temporary abandonment of the idea, long cherished by the artificial intelligence community, that the digital computer could interact with its human users in a cognitively symbiotic manner (Winograd and Flores 1986). In its place, they proposed an organizational metaphor which positioned the computer as a tool for social communication. For them, there was little to be gained from further analogizing computation and human thought – in fact it distracted from the essential task of accounting for what computing devices do in a context of human practice. For us, the same thing can now be said about the metaphor of the computer as a tool for learning or even as a site for interaction. The questions most needing to be asked about how to optimize e-learning in the university are no longer inspired by theories of cognitive development, or models of collaborative knowledge construction. They arise from the recognition that e-learning technologies have taken their place, along with a great diversity of other social and cultural factors, as sites in which practices of 'doing university work' are carried out. In particular, they are sites in which linguistic communication goes on, predominantly in writing, in the service of relations of authority among participants. In short, they are sites of literacy practice.

3

The social literacies of learning with technologies

Robin Goodfellow

In Chapter 2, I critiqued what I called the 'tools-for-learning' metaphor in which learning technologies are viewed as a means of facilitating, amplifying or extending cognitive processes, both individual and distributed. This metaphor has underpinned the development of a pedagogy for e-learning which focuses on the design of environments, activities and tools for dialogue or interaction between people or between people and machines. Such a pedagogy is consistent with a constructivist understanding of the cognitive and social nature of human learning, and is appropriate to educational policies that aim to gear university learning to participation in a 'knowledge economy' in which knowledge is collaboratively constructed and commoditized. However, pedagogical designs and activities that are based solely around the affordances of technologies as learning tools, and which do not take account of the role in learning of the identities (individual and institutional) and wider social practices of the human participants, are always likely to be contested by some of these participants, with possibly detrimental effects for the learning community as a whole. The alternative metaphor that I proposed is that of the technologies as 'sites of practice' in which activity and meaning-making are shaped by social relations deriving from the wider social and institutional setting, as well as from the technical arena of educational interaction. In this chapter, I develop this perspective and explore some of the social and ideological dimensions in which university teaching and learning and the use of e-learning technologies operate. In particular, I examine the role of discourses about literacy in shaping the way we think about learning and communicating with technologies, a theme that will then be taken up by Mary, in Chapter 4, in the specific context of academic literacies.

The VLE as a site of institutional practice

The World Wide Web has turned into the 'killer application' for educational technology, just as Collis (1996) predicted it would. However, it was never a specifically 'educational' technology, and participants in other arenas of social practice (commerce, government, community services) took it up too, initially in the same *ad hoc* manner as universities did, but eventually developing characteristic ways of using it more systematically to carry out their business. Some of these commercially developed practices have since been introduced into educational use, for example, the personalization of websites so that they can store information about users and their preferences, and use this to customize the services they provide (see Weller 2007 for a more detailed discussion of this in the context of learning 'portals'). One example, however, of an activity greatly enabled by the Web, which has developed as a very specifically educational practice, is the use of 'discussion boards' (or 'discussion forums') for conducting tutorials and collaborative learning activities, a practice that has largely displaced the use of email for these purposes. Discussion boards, prior to the Web, required users to install 'client' programs on their computers in order to create the interfaces which were used to display messages and message lists, and to manage reply and other functions associated with online discussion. With web-based boards they could use the same browser software to conduct discussions that they used to access other web pages. But web-based discussion still requires institutional investment in systems at the web server end that are additional to baseline email systems, and the discussion areas also need to be actively structured by developers at course- or subject department-level before they can be used by students, so it is interesting that they were seen as so much more amenable to tutorial work than generic email systems. The reason is probably that the discussion board much more closely approximates to the physical classroom than does email, in a number of ways. The environment can be primed by the teacher to facilitate a certain kind of interaction, such as a lesson or a debate, as they would do in a physical classroom; learners are required to 'turn up' there by logging on to the discussion area (whereas email just arrives on their desktops); discussion boards have a much more apparent public and many-to-many dimension (in fact email lists are just as public but notoriously create the illusion of being one-to-one); the content of discussion is 'owned' by the group in a more evident way, as aspects of the organization and storage of messages are taken out of the hands of individual contributors. All these characteristics contribute to the ability of the discussion board to reproduce the classroom in many of its essential features, and perhaps account for its popularity in e-learning. These technologies have developed as sites of a particular kind of social practice which is only partly determined by the medium itself, and is mainly shaped by existing habits of interaction reflecting conventions of classroom authority, social relations and social literacy.

One could consider the concept of people 'attending' a virtual classroom, via a university website and an electronic discussion board, as yet another version of the tools-for-learning metaphor, one that has had a strong appeal for practitioners in both face-to-face and distance education, and one that an entire psychological and pedagogical rationale has developed around, as we saw in the previous chapter. This metaphor of attendance can in fact be used to account for the whole configuration of web-based learning material, plus online discussion, plus (more recently) student support 'portal', which today comprises many institutional VLEs, as is discussed further in Chapter 4. The public and professional rhetoric of the VLE is about new modes of flexible lifelong learning, at any time and from any place, but the underlying trope still positions learners and teachers in traditional configurations – classes, lecture halls, examination rooms, courses – just as university education has always done, although with the added convenience of virtual delocation and flexible asynchronous time. This re-creation of conventional configurations is not due to some failure of imagination on the part of VLE designers, it is a consequence of the fact that university learning remains institutionalized, and structures of admittance and attendance are necessary to the survival of the university system and to socialized higher education in general. From the overhead projector to the VLE, the technologies deployed help to construct the experience of teaching and learning at university as one of attendance: at a high-status social institution, in the company of prestigious individuals, involved with the creation and transfer of cultural capital (Bourdieu's term for legitimate knowledge of one kind or other, expressed in language use, manners, orientations and dispositions to knowing, according to Jenkins 1992: 85 and 116) via the texts and literacies (systems of authoring, owning and appropriating texts) of the academy and, more recently, the professions. In this way the technologies of the VLE function as sites of practice at the wider institutional and social levels too.

The digital native and the discourse of 'literacy crisis'

By and large, the constructivist and collaborative approaches to online learning that I reviewed in Chapter 2, while broadly 'socio-cultural' in concept, do not engage directly with the institutional or wider cultural context of the interaction that they seek to generate. This is both consequence and cause of a tendency to treat learners as autonomous agents, whose communication needs and preferences alone determine the way teaching and learning proceed and the learning outcomes that result. With the proliferation of electronic communication practices developed in non-educational contexts, particularly in areas of commercial and recreational use of the Internet, the needs and preferences of university learners are increasingly being shaped by practices borrowed from non-study contexts, for example, the use of search engines rather than libraries to locate information. The coming to maturity of a generation of students whose reading and writing and general communication practices are predominantly conducted outside formal educational contexts, via screens and keyboards of one kind or another, has led to the emergence of a discourse of the 'digital native' which is being brought to bear on the literacy practices of the classroom. Learner preferences in this rhetoric are constructed as actively antipathetic to the traditional print-based communication of schools and universities.

Lankshear and Knobel (2003) refer to the term 'digital native' as having been introduced by John Perry Barlow in an interview in *Australian Personal Computer* in 1995 (Tunbridge 1995). The underlying notion of a generation born to be users of electronic media has been well rehearsed by a number of authors – (Rushkoff 1994; Negroponte 1995), but it has most recently been popularized by Prensky (2001). Prensky's construction of the digital native is a young person brought up with computers and the Internet and constantly exposed to the Web, TV and Internet marketing, video gaming and digital networking. As they have spent far more time in front of the TV or computer screen than reading books or newspapers, they inevitably, according to Prensky, think in a qualitatively different kind of way than earlier generations raised on print-based communication. New competences and dispositions have replaced the linear logical thinking of the print-literate, including increased speed of response, capacity to multi-task, intuitive grasping of visual and associative subtexts, orientation to play and to creating connections with large and loosely networked groups of like-minded others.

In the more simplistic celebratory and futuristic rhetorics of e-learning, the educational implications of teaching these digital native or 'E generation' (Krause 2006) students are seen as simply a matter of designing for the new skills and dispositions, for example, by replacing instructional task-sequencing with random access, and, in Prensky's (2001) own words, by the complete elimination of 'any language that even *smacked* of education' (so as not to alienate the natives). Although the technologies and their associated practices may eventually have implications for 'ethics, politics, sociology, languages and other things that go with them', as Prensky notes, the main challenge that they pose for education is usually seen as methodological: a matter of finding ways to present existing curriculum content using the new media favoured by the students, but without any radical change to the curriculum itself. However, to a non-educational audience the idea of a generation of learners whose brains are actually different, because they have grown up looking at moving images rather than reading static print, can appear as deeply threatening to an established order of social value and achievement. The British neuro-biologist and peer, Susan Greenfield articulated this perception in a speech about future education policy to the House of Lords on 20 April 2006 (Hansard, HL (series 5), vol. 680, cols 1219–22).[1] Greenfield expressed considerable concern that new ways of processing information characteristic of the digital multimedia environments that children are increasingly exposed to online might be adversely affecting basic cognitive abilities traditionally developed through reading, such as memory,

---

[1] http://www.publications.parliament.uk/pa/ld199900/ldhansrd/pdvn/lds06/text/60420–18.htm#60420–18_spopq0 (accessed January 2007).

imagination and creativity. Greenfield is no luddite – the ostensible purpose of her rhetoric was actually to bring pressure on the government to increase its investment in research into learning technologies in general and her own institute, FutureLab, in particular. But she tapped into a vein of popular anxiety about 'screen culture' when she characterized it (quoting the journalist, Kevin Kelly) as 'a world of constant flux, of endless sound bites, quick cuts and half-baked ideas . . . a flow of gossip titbits, news headlines and floating first impressions' (col. 1219). She associated multimedia environments with 'immediate sensory content' accessed at the expense of reflection or imaginative connection, and denigrated any learning that could be done via this medium. For her, the children exposed to it were simply 'having an experience' rather than learning. Furthermore, she warned that the decline of reading in favour of this kind of sensory experience might result in the loss of some of the facilities of memory, and even in the loss of imagination altogether, 'that mysterious and special cognitive achievement that until now has always made the book so very much better than the film' (col. 1220). Although the speech was couched in scientific terms, it was the speech of a politician rather than a scientist, as the real force of the argument she was making was moral rather than scientific and the message subsequently taken up by the national news media was that the Internet is changing our children's brains for the worse (Ashley 2006). Without offering any direct evidence of a decline in reading standards, Greenfield was nevertheless able to play on concerns familiar from earlier eras about the way technologies might interfere with our personal and social development, how the telephone would stop people visiting each other, how the cinema would affect reading habits, how television would kill the art of conversation, how hypertext would destroy the art of writing. Most significantly she re-raised the spectre of literacy crisis that repeatedly haunted English-speaking societies in the twentieth century: the fear that modern media might directly condition our learning in adverse ways, with far-reaching effects on traditional literacy and on society as a whole.

Street (1995: 132–5) has described the belief that the skills, competences and dispositions involved in reading and writing are natural and universal attributes of individual cognitive development as an 'autonomous' model of literacy (further discussed by Mary in Chapter 4). Autonomous models of literacy inform a great deal of pedagogical practice at all levels of the education system, from the teaching of reading in schools to the teaching of information literacy in universities. They tend to imply that becoming literate is principally a matter of gaining mastery of the systems and technical modes of communication available: the pen, the alphabet, the keyboard, the screen and the database. The digital native discourse is typical of this viewpoint, arguing that systems and modes of communication that are the products of very recent technological developments are favoured by the young over the more traditional systems employed by the schools, and that they, therefore, become literate in the use of these new systems rather than in conventional reading and writing and develop cognitive, or information processing, capabilities that are significantly different from those developed through print literacy. This, essentially operational, view of literacy as set of cognitive skills and dispositions has a long history and its relationship with the technologies of print is deeply embedded in social and educational practice. It is owed, in large part, to the work of Ong (1982) and others, who argued influentially for a qualitative distinction between literacy and orality, and for the view that written literacy as cognitive development is on a higher intellectual plane than oral communication, that someone who can read and write is cognitively and socially better equipped than someone who cannot, and that civilizations that have developed written language are more advanced than those that have not. This model of literacy can be seen as reflecting social relations in industrially developed societies, in which reading and writing underpin a whole range of communication activities that are of social and cultural value, and where there is often a direct link between higher levels of written literacy and membership of the more prosperous and dominant social classes. Intellectual achievement recognized by success in written examinations still constitutes a clear sign of class and status, and universities are an integral part of this process. In Britain, for example, a university degree, still awarded primarily as recognition of achievement in written literacy, is thought to confer on its holder both social distinction and a premium on lifetime earnings estimated by the UK government at around £400,000 (Hoare 2002).

Traditional print literacy has indeed become one of the principal means by which we define ourselves, both individually and as a society, as civilized. A belief in the inherent cognitive and social value of written literacy has also led some communities to go beyond the mastering of the operational means of communication, to develop particular ways of thinking, speaking and behaving intended to distinguish literate people as educated, 'cultured', intelligent people, who are of social worth, possessors of cultural capital. Because of this highly valued cultural dimension of written literacy the suggestion that reading and writing standards might be dropping, or that they are being threatened by new technologies, or that practices are changing in unpredictable ways, is always a cause of concern, if not panic, about what is going on in schools and colleges. The controversy that surrounded the apparent discovery of high levels of illiteracy among American adults in the early 1970s (Crowley 1995) resulted in the reinstatement of compulsory composition classes, which had been dropped by many universities after student protests in the 1960s. That 'literacy crisis' spread to Australia and the UK, and was renewed with the publication of a now-famous article entitled 'Why Johnny Can't Write' in *Newsweek* in 1975 (Shiels 1975), which blamed an 'alarming' decline in reading and writing on television viewing and 'creative' teaching. These 'crises' also implicated other educational, ideological and technological issues which were not confined to the classroom. In the course of the American controversy, for example, there were politically motivated attacks on 'liberals, intellectuals, immigrants and the irreligious, as well as criticisms aimed at TV and the IT industry' (Lankshear and

Knobel 2003: 6–7). The predictability of the recurring public outcry against declining literacy standards, regardless of the evidence, suggests, according to Lankshear and Knobel (2003), that public concern about reading and writing might in fact be a proxy for other, less easily understood, social changes that are perhaps not so directly linked to educational practice – worry about new employment skills that are necessitated by structural changes in the labour market, for example; or, to bring us back to the present discussion, moral concern about new recreational practices emerging among the youthful natives of the net generation.

Digital literacy – cultural and critical dimensions

While public concern over reading and writing standards and the effects of new technological practices explicitly asserts the wider established values of a social hierarchy based on print communication, the digital native rhetoric does something similar for the values of the electronic generation. It does this by identifying them as the generation on which our future prosperity in the technologized knowledge economy depends, a generation whose education requires changes to the 'outmoded' literacy practices of formal teaching. Discourses, such as this, display cultural dimensions that have implications for our approach to literacy that go beyond the individual skills and communication preferences involved. These cultural dimensions are often realized in forms of social action that are embarked on as remedies for the literacy crises that are perceived to threaten us, a return to 'basic instruction' in reading and writing, for example, or increased investment in scientific research into 'the problem', or the official recognition of the legitimacy (and marketability) of young people's recreational media practices.

A theorized view of literacy as cultural practice that recognizes these dimensions has been developing among educationalists since the 1970s when it arose partly in reaction to the functional teaching that accompanied the repeated 'literacy crises', and partly as an integral strand of the 'turn to the social' that came to characterize thinking across the social sciences from the 1960s onwards (see Gee 2000 for an account of this paradigm change). The work of Scribner and Cole (1981), who proposed that the origin of mental abilities was more likely to be found in the practices of Western schooling rather than in the acquisition of a specific kind of written literacy, and others who explored the role of communities in determining the values that were attached to literacy practices of different kinds (e.g., Heath 1983; Street 1984; and see Chapter 4) was the basis for a movement that contested the popular notion of literacy as an essentially individual accomplishment, objectively measurable against a universally recognized scale of competence. This movement issued a critical challenge to the taken-for-granted superiority of particular kinds of written literacy and the assumed connection between these and the higher cognitive functions. It raised questions about the part played in literate communication by aspects of context, such as the relationship between reader and writer, their location, other kinds of texts involved, the media used, and a whole range of other social factors that could be considered to be part of the message and its interpretation.

Street has used the term 'ideological' to encapsulate the central role that literacies play in systems of social valuation and the negotiation of power relations, and to mark autonomous models as necessarily inadequate to explain issues and problems to do with reading and writing in social contexts (Street 1995: 151). Ideologies, assumptions that directly or indirectly legitimize existing power relations, are often hidden in the language we use, masquerading as common-sense or everyday talk, as Mary discussed in Chapter 1. An important function of pedagogies for literacy, which adopt an ideological model, is to develop a critique of the very practices that are their focus of study, enabling the hidden assumptions and the power relations they support, to be made evident and the processes by which these power relations came to be established to be understood. Many researchers and practitioners associated with the composition and rhetorical studies fields in the USA, concerned with the cultural nature of literacy and its relation to class, gender and ethnic identities in the classroom, have taken up the challenge of this critical turn, seeking to teach their students to reflect on the nature of the discourses they encounter inside and outside the classroom, and to become capable of 'critiquing ideology to imagine possibilities for social transformation' (LeCourt 1998: 276). Some of these practitioners were among the earliest experimenters with computer-assisted learning, in the form of word-processing tools, early hypertext systems, email and text chat (see Selfe and Hilligoss 1994), believing that computer-based activities could be sites in which conventional classroom discourses could be contested, as the authority of teachers and authors is undermined by the destabilizing effects of digital media on the production of text. At the same time, other educationalists turned the critical lens which had been used to problematize conventional academic literacy practices back onto the technologies, arguing for an understanding of the cultural and historical attitudes, values and conditions that shape their use. This 'critical technological literacy' (Selfe 1999) attempted to make explicit all the values underlying the discursive and communicative acts that are carried out in digital environments and sought to bring the literacies approach out of the writing and composition classrooms and place it at the heart of all teaching and learning with technology.

I explored the critical dimension of online communication for myself in a study of distance learners attempting to negotiate norms of interaction in an asynchronous electronic discussion environment (Goodfellow 2004b). In this study, the messaging practices of one highly operationally competent student were experienced as culturally intimidating by others, who were unable to meet the standards of quantity and erudition of opinion that they felt were being set. An intervention by the teacher, intended to persuade the overperforming student to modify his practices, exposed a conflict between the 'educational' values of the course developers, who viewed the online discussion as a means to an end, and the 'professional communication' values espoused by some of its student participants, including the one who was the source of the problem, for whom the online discussion was itself the purpose of their activity. This conflict eventually began to be expressed in the form of personal criticism as well as general debate, with the result that one of the intimidated participants ceased to take any further part in the discussion. My argument from this study was that in making explicit the ideological dimension of course literacy practices – the way that certain forms of interaction were constructed as legitimate – the event had brought the power relations between the university and its students into the open and made them available for critique and contestation by those who did not necessarily accept them. The difficulty that many of the participants seemed to experience with textual debate at this level, and the subsequent recourse to personal criticism, may have been a result of impatience at the additional time required to engage in it, but it was also, in my view, a consequence of the fact that the course did not explicitly recognize the critical dimension of its online literacy practices. In a subsequent study carried out across courses in the same distance learning programme (Goodfellow 2005b) I looked for evidence of learners taking up critical stances on course literacy practices, as they were encouraged to do in a supplementary online writing support resource, and found that few individuals were prepared to do so. The majority preferred to reproduce the 'dominant' views of writing as represented by official course and university teaching and study support texts, which paid little heed to the particular nature of the writing that these students were required to produce in the context of online communication.

It is in the nature of dominant ideologies that they are problematic to contest, that they 'close down' discourses, as Fairclough (2001: 207) puts it, by codifying the language that can be used to dispute them. An example of this is the way that many university programmes in the UK, following the recommendations of the Dearing Report (NCIHE 1997; see Chapter 1), present the online activities that students engage in as developing specific communication and group-working skills which are assumed to be transferable across the many contexts of lifelong learning. Positioning online communication as a skill in this way serves institutional agendas wishing to present e-learning as promoting employability very well, but it obscures the context-dependent dimension of electronic texts, and works against engaging learners in a reflexive critique of their own literacy practices. In particular, it works against the conceptualization of texts generated in online university classrooms as a specifically *written* form of social practice, inheriting the same ideological dimension as other, more obviously power-related practices, such as essay-writing and marking, and academic publication (Lea forthcoming).

An ideological model of literacy, together with attention to the critical dimension of literacy practice, is what underpins the literacies approach to e-learning developed here. I am drawing on the relatively recent tradition of exploration of literacy as social practice, and on fields of research known as New Literacy Studies (Street 2003) and academic literacies (see Chapter 4). A critical framing is inherent in much of the recent work on literacy as applied to educational issues at school level; for example, there has been a significant attempt in the 'multiliteracies' movement (New London Group 1996; Cope and Kalantzis 1999) to influence the teaching of literacy (particularly in Australia) along lines which recognize new kinds of power differential accompanying the growing cultural diversity of school learners in heterogeneous societies, and the spread of new communications media based on digital technologies. Also derived from the multiliteracies perspective is a parallel strand of 'new literacies' theorizing based on the metaphor of the digitally 'at home' (Negroponte 1995; Lankshear and Knobel 2004). This foregrounds the significance of new technology and argues for a transformation of educational practice in response to an emerging new epistemological order based on electronic communication, much as did the pioneers of online collaborative learning, discussed in Chapter 2. Lankshear and Knobel (2003) claim that their interest is not only in those literacies that involve ICTs – they also talk more generally about new practices, such as scenario planning for political decision-making – but their key discussion of different 'mindsets' relating to the way new technologies are perceived by students and teachers draws very largely on the same distinction between technological natives and non-natives that I discussed above. This and similar viewpoints have found pedagogical expression under a variety of labels, such as 'techno-literacy' (Lankshear *et al.* 2000), 'silicon literacies' (Snyder 2002) and 'new literacies' (Lankshear and Knobel 2003). These framings pose their own challenge to the university's traditional concern with disciplinary knowledge, and at the same time they also pose a challenge to our own approach to e-learning as a site of educational practice because of their focus on the technologies, and on the modality of communication rather than the nature of the social practices it enacts. These perspectives, which I will refer to collectively as 'new media' literacies, build on the theme of the digital insider, and on the cultural significance of Internet communication. In adopting a social practice perspective on the use of popular digital media, they go beyond the kind of concern about the impact of screen-based communication on the information processing capacities of students that Greenfield was expressing, to propose more fundamental, structural implications for education in the modern age. In particular, they assert what Kress has called a 'tectonic' shift from page to screen, with ever increasing importance accorded to the visual image in communication of all kinds (Kress 1998: 58; Kress and van Leeuwen 2001). The growing diversity and centrality of media in educational interaction has given rise to a proposal for a 'design curriculum' to replace the traditional academic concern with critique (New London Group 1996; Kress 2003a), in which written language is seen as just one of a range of semiotic modes available to the learner for the construction of meaning. These ideas resonate strongly with the some of the more radical visions for the development of e-learning (e.g. Downes 2006) that are being generated in the current drive for technological innovation in many universities, as I will discuss later.

'New media' literacies and the design curriculum

'New media' literacies thinking asserts that the use of new media and multi-modal forms of communication necessarily entails the development of new social literacies that will eventually come to supersede conventional language-based literacies (Kress 2003a; Lankshear and Knobel 2003). This notion is grounded in an analysis that characterizes the social and economic relations and technologies of communication in the post-modern age as undergoing a 'revolution' (Kress 2003a). The argument develops a theme introduced by the New London Group (1996), to the effect that education is being reshaped by workplaces, markets, media and lifestyle groupings, and that literacy pedagogy needs to reflect a new diversity of learner identities and technologies of representation. The 'design curriculum' principle proposed by Kress argues that in such periods of social and technological change, learners can no longer be regarded as users of stable systems of knowledge and its representation, and have to be seen as remakers and transformers of the representational resources themselves. He describes this as 'the orchestrating and remaking of representational resources in the service of frameworks and models that express the makers' intentions in shaping the social and cultural environment' (Kress 1998: 76–7). He specifically contrasts the new focus on design with the established academic principle of critique, which he argues is necessarily backward-looking, reflecting on the way that things have previously been done and attempting to shape the future via a modification of the past. The superseding of critique he sees as particularly implied by the growing domination of the visual mode in modern communication, and the increasing power of the logic of the image over that of the written text.

At the heart of the new media literacies approach, therefore, and at the heart of the challenge to academic practices posed by the design curriculum, are new operational skills developed around technical facilities that allow the everyday creation and exchange of images, video and audio, as well as text. Lankshear and Knobel suggest that these new skills are being used to create entirely new forms of cultural identity expressed as entirely new forms of literate practice. The prominence of pictures and graphics on contemporary web pages, weblogs and other personal spaces, for example, is argued to be evidence of a significant change in the habitual presentation of self to an audience, moving away from the linearity of textual description and towards the immediacy of visual design. New social literacy practices are also observed in other online practices, such as the ranking of individual websites and blogs, in terms of popularity measured by the number of 'hits' received as people access these pages and, hopefully, consume the information they contain, thus conferring social distinction on those whose individual spaces gain significant prominence. These practices, it is argued, create a form of 'attention economy' (Goldhaber 1997), in which people compete for audience, and gain social status in proportion to their success in attracting visitors to their pages. Rating systems are also ways for the unknown and unseen participants in social media exchanges to create and preserve reputations. Online trading sites, such as eBay, or communities formed around the exchange of valued information, such as the computer technologists' site Slashdot (http://slashdot.org/), encourage participants to rate each others' contribution to business or to discussion, in order to ensure their continued valuing of the exchange. An eBay 'seller' who failed to accurately describe goods offered for sale, for example, would be given a low rating by the dissatisfied buyer and would then find it difficult to attract further people with whom to trade. Other new media practices cited by Lankshear and Knobel as significant for the development of new practices that may eventually give rise to new forms of literacy include: contributing to e-zines (online reader-generated magazines); collaboration in multimedia project spaces; and camcorder counter-surveillance (e.g. the use of videocams to 'spy' on the police).

Online practices such as these have been made technically possible because, whereas the original architecture of the World Wide Web made use of protocols that enabled the users of 'server' systems to create information for the users of 'client' systems to access, the current generation of Internet technologies includes web services which enable clients to exchange information created by themselves. This development, known variously as the 'read/write web' or, (at the time of writing) 'Web 2.0' (O'Reilly 2005), has coincided with the mass availability of mobile phones, digital cameras and audio devices, and a major expansion in the telecommunications bandwidth available to ordinary users in their homes and workplaces. The result has been the rapid spread of new practices of electronic personal publishing and remote 'social networking', as typified by websites, such as YouTube, MySpace, Facebook and many others (Alexander 2006) which provide free personal spaces and support for individuals to create websites and journals (blogs) on which they can publish multimedia content created by themselves, create links to the spaces and content of other individuals and groups, and host discussions with selected other users around topics of mutual interest. Collectively known as 'social media', these services are used by ordinary users primarily for maintaining social networks with friends and colleagues, but they are also exploited by advertisers and the news and entertainment industries for the promotion and distribution of products and the collection of market information. News Corporation, the owners of MySpace, for example, projected a revenue from advertising, share of royalties, and sale of specific services of $200 million in 2006 (Hansell 2006), based on more than 70 million registered users (although a relatively small proportion of these are significantly active online). YouTube, on which people can publish homemade video content of all kinds, is now being further popularized by mainstream media, such as newspapers and broadcast TV. This has been part of what has been called a 'torrent' of user-generated content and informal social networking (Naughton 2007) brought about by the new generation of web technology.

The increasing popularity of social media websites, which are differentiated from each other by scale of use, the kinds of content sharing they support and the particular social groups they engage (Alexander 2006 discusses about thirty of them, and refers to 'hundreds' of others) has caused a major shake-up in business practice in established areas of the media and entertainment industries, such as music, books, TV and newspapers. Small-scale user-generated content has come to rival for popularity cultural artefacts, such as blockbuster books and hit TV shows produced on a large scale and marketed to mass audiences in the conventional manner (Anderson 2005). Furthermore, 'social bookmarking' practices, such as collecting links to shareable resources and 'tagging' them (labelling the collection with an intuitively meaningful term or expression that other users can then adopt to align it with their own collections), have introduced new possibilities for individuals to integrate their tastes and interests with those of others, leading to the development of interest groups capable of growing into significant 'niche' markets for cultural products in their own right. University courses, as cultural artefacts themselves, stand in a similar market relationship to emerging practices of social networking and user-generated content, as do the products of the media industries. The millions of users of social media clearly represent a sizeable potential market for the purveyors of e-learning, particularly as many of them are thought to have demographic profiles similar to those of populations identified by governments as the targets of the effort to widen participation in higher education (e.g. first-generation entrants, ethnic groups, lower-income groups and other 'non-traditional' students).

But more immediate concerns for university e-learning practitioners than marketing are posed by the social media and the dispositions of digital natives, in the pedagogical arena. These concerns are intensified by the pressure from new media literacies theorists and from some e-learning developers to regard social media practices as new literacies integral to the development of design competencies within a new curriculum. But there are important issues still unresolved about the ways in which the new domains of user-generated content and peer rating can be integrated with the institutional practices of the VLE that I discussed in the previous section. For example, initial indications from small-scale research, carried out by the JISC in 2006, were that digitally sophisticated students in UK universities use a variety of web services for activities related to their studies and that they go beyond the 'learning content' provided by their courses and use web technologies to find, manage and produce their own content. They also use each other as a study support network, communicating via a variety of systems (phone, email, MSN, etc.). However, the same research also suggests that many of these students have a 'marked lack of enthusiasm' for the institutional VLEs provided by their universities (Conole *et al.* 2006: 100), possibly because these official systems are not used consistently across courses and because they fit only marginally with students' study requirements, for example, in searching for materials (Conole *et al.* 2006: 104). Some of the students' antipathy to the institutional virtual spaces is also, in all likelihood, because these represent the conventional practices and authority structures of the university, while user-generated content and social networking embody an alternative and more informal set of values. New media literacies theorists argue that Internet-based communication practices are important new forms of literacy for the specific groups of people who engage with them. They point to the engagement of under–25-year-olds with MySpace, for example, and to the influence that this network has on contemporary popular culture, as many pop music and TV stars now use the site to publicize themselves and their work. MySpace users constitute themselves as 'insider' groups involved in the construction of new, informal, hierarchies reflecting their shared values as participants in non-traditional forms of cultural exchange. The oppositional stance taken to these sites by some schools and local educational authorities, which have banned the use of them by pupils during school time, reinforces this perception. Lankshear and Knobel argue that the failure of schools to engage as insiders with this and other youth phenomena, while at the same time attempting to use new technologies to reproduce old-fashioned, non-electronic literacy forms, is a failure of education systems at the most fundamental level. But at the same time they suggest that these new literacies have the capacity to resist the continuing dominance of institutions, governments and corporations (Lankshear and Knobel 2003: 33–45). This theme of resistance resonates with the viewpoint of Downes and others who envisage the challenging and eventual radical transformation of institutionalized education through the practices of e-learning. In Downes's (2006) words:

> The model of e-learning as being a type of content, produced by publishers, organized and structured into courses, and consumed by students, is turned on its head. Insofar as there is content, it is used rather than read ... And insofar as there is structure, it is more likely to resemble a language or a conversation rather than a book or a manual.

While these views are highly speculative, and have not been translated into any major e-learning design initiatives in any university that I am aware of (at the time of writing), they nevertheless crystallize the relation between the new media literacies thinking and the dominant rhetoric of e-learning. Downes contrasts 'using' with 'reading' and 'language/conversation' with 'book or manual', and in doing so makes it clear that the underlying issues are to do with literacy practices, but despite the ideological rationale the new media literacies approach continues to characterize these practices primarily in terms of the modality of the communication they involve (i.e. the channel or the material form of the message), rather than the particular forms of social action these enact. Lankshear and Knobel's (2003: 44) valorizing of 'communication guerrilla' practices typified, for example, by the hoaxing of journalists, flouting of copyright on downloaded music and counter-surveillance videos, celebrates the ability of the young people concerned to take control of the technologies and turn them to narratives of resistance to corporatism and global capital. But as examples of social practice – of 'emerging youth cultures' – these are almost completely overshadowed by more recent and more widespread practices, such as the dissemination of jokey and trivial video clips (e.g. CCTV footage of people falling over) on YouTube, the posting of hoax stories on Wikinews and other open sites where anyone can post a 'news' story, the bullying and 'flaming' (abusing in electronic text) of unpopular peers on MySpace, the sexualizing of young women's self-presentation on a variety of social networking sites, the prominence of commercial advertising in almost all virtual spaces, and many other examples of ephemeral and uncritical forms of social practice associated with the spread of Internet communication.

Moreover, while social media interaction undoubtedly engages its users in a range of multimodal operational skills, including those involved in reading and writing online, design, in Kress's sense of 'shaping the social and cultural environment', as a distinctly literate practice is often marginal to online activity. As research at Columbia University has shown (Salganik *et al.* 2006), the 'attention economy' of the Internet is as likely to generate an unconscious alignment with majority taste as it is to stimulate original forms of self-identification. In the competition for rankings of cultural content, such as pop songs, for example, it is generally assumed that audiences will recognize quality in some products, according to their own tastes, and value these more than others which lack the same quality. The Columbia research showed that American teenagers downloading, discussing and ranking new songs, via social networking sites, aligned their tastes to each other's in a way that did not ultimately relate to any objective standard of quality of the content. The researchers concluded that the demands of evaluating a large number of competing songs led the majority of the teenagers to attend only to those that others had already rated. It is not that such 'herd' behaviour is all that happens on the social media sites, as there is clearly a great deal of constructive and creative user content generation going on. However, now that the social media technologies are becoming increasingly normalized and accessible, the equal facility with which they may be used to perpetuate practices that are at best conformist and at worst trivializing or even oppressive, suggests that the scope they offer for the reshaping of the social and cultural environment may be more limited than the e-learning radicals or the new media literacies theorists acknowledge.

It can be argued that radical new media literacy agendas for education, such as multiliteracies and the design curriculum, in their concern to problematize traditional educational practice in conditions of post-modernity actually run the risk of buying into larger and more pernicious discourses of capitalism and globalization (Matthews 2005). This is because at the heart of the conceptualization of 'social futures' (New London Group 1996) in an age dominated by communication technology is a rationale about the relationship between learning and the knowledge economy that takes as given the role of higher education in providing 'marketable workplace expertise, abilities, innovation, and creativity' for the purposes of commercial competition (Matthews 2005: 221). However, new literacy practices are not simply responses to economic and technological change, they are the products of cultures, histories and politics. Matthews demonstrates the way that cartoons have been used to critique contemporary political themes, such as the 'war on terrorism'. She argues that these 'new' literacies of visual design can be put to the service of a critical pedagogical engagement with political discourses that 'disperse power and construct identities' (Matthews 2005: 221). This argument for the value of both critique and design in the making of meaning in new media environments is one that has particular relevance to the literacies of e-learning in the university, as critical thinking is central to student learning and academic practice.

New and traditional literacies in university e-learning practice

The same focus on modality rather than social practice, that I critiqued in regard to the new media literacies discourse above, is also evident in the new media discourses that currently influence e-learning practices in the university, particularly in the domains of 'IT literacy' and 'information literacy', as we will discuss in the context of the case studies described in Chapter 5. In the report on students' experiences of technologies, referred to earlier (Conole *et al.* 2006: 5), the researchers claim that new technologies are producing new working and studying practices that are changing the way that knowledge is gathered, used and created, and shifting the nature of the skills exercised towards the 'higher levels of Bloom's taxonomy' (analysis, synthesis and evaluation, according to Bloom *et al.* 1956). However, there is very little evidence provided that attests to the students' use of the new knowledge and 'skills' that have been produced, in the context of their studies. From the point of view of those who are already committed to a belief in paradigmatic change in epistemologies and pedagogies driven by the mere availability of new technologies, the collection of such evidence can perhaps wait until the new practices are sufficiently established. From a more critical perspective, however, the successful establishment of these technologies as new sites of academic practice will depend on their adaptability to existing systems of social relations in the university, such as those that govern the formal assessment of the new 'skills' and knowledge. To be taken up as sites of new academic literacy practice these technologies will have to be put to the service of disciplinary as well as innovatory epistemologies.

In universities, the spread of new multimodal communication practices and innovative approaches to design is involved in a complex and ongoing interaction with existing and deeply embedded academic literacy practices based on writing and on critique. The integration of e-learning should not, therefore, be seen as a 'revolution' in university literacies, rather a gradual process of assimilation of techniques and accommodation to values and aspirations. Well-established institutional practices in university education, such as selection, assessment and accreditation, do not interact in a straight-forward way with the new practices of Internet sociability and content generation. Visual imagery, for example, may be the principal means of gaining attention on the Internet, but written text is still the principal means of information exchange for most bloggers, and writing is still the key activity for the majority of academic disciplines, where it is regarded as one of the most significant material forms that reasoning can take. As Bayne (2006: 1) puts it 'the linear, logically-developing scholarly text, with its hierarchical structure and build towards conclusion, is still the primary expression of the academic mind'. This makes written text the principal route to acceptance into both blogging and academic communities, including, I might add, the community of new media literacies theorists. In universities in the anglo-phone world writing continues to be the primary mode of student assessment, too, despite the technology-led search for a more cost-effective alternative, simply because it carries ideological markers which make it more important than other forms of discourse. In many subject areas the development of a student's writing ability has come to be seen as practically synonymous with their acquisition of knowledge in that subject. We might argue that the assessment of student writing encapsulates the power relations that exist at the heart of formal university education, as assessment and accreditation are highly significant arenas of social practice which have had centuries of consolidation. They are also sites of contestation between new media and established institutional processes as the pressure to streamline examination systems, in order to manage greater numbers of students at lower costs, has opened the way for the application of new technologies, such as automatic assignment marking, and the adoption of simplified formats, such as multiple choice questionnaires. Now there is a moral panic about plagiarism as students themselves turn to technology and the Internet in the face of the demands being made on them and the scarcity of resources. Many universities, understanding that they undermine the public credibility of their accreditation procedures at their peril, are looking for technical 'solutions' in the form of anti-plagiarism software, while others turn back to conventional examinations and to established practices, such as projects and portfolios, using technology primarily for administrative rather than evaluative purposes.

University libraries are also sites of complex interaction between new media and established process. As key repositories (gatekeepers even) of academic practice, libraries have a keen interest in the intersection of technology with academic literacies, as conventionally understood. However, the task for them is not yet seen as one of adapting existing conventions of sourcing, referencing, validation, etc. to new digital practices, such as social bookmarking and weblog design, but rather the other way round. Voyager, the University of Auckland's system for inducting new students to library practices (http://voyager.auckland.ac.nz/), is a good example of the overlaying of contemporary informal cultural literacies, such as are embodied in conventions of visual design, on more traditional academic literacy practices, such as looking up references, finding sources, etc. This system is a webbased tutorial which interfaces to the University of Auckland library website. The library homepage itself is of a conventional design, with the standard academic library menus and search facilities: catalogue, booking forms, journals, access to library learning material, etc. The Voyager tutorial, however, is in the form of a multimedia graphic novel which tells the story of Jay, a student new to the university, and his efforts to find various resources on his course reading list, and an animated-screen tutorial taking the user through the stages of performing the various kinds of search through the library catalogue that Jay attempts. The contrast between the two modes of interaction with the website is quite striking. The Jay story is a horizontally scrolling comic strip which uses illustration, photo-montage, music and ambient sound, text (talk bubbles in colloquial language) and a pop-up glossary, to address the theme of being 'adrift upon a sea of information' – a voyaging motif realized through Maori and Pacific cultural images and symbols. Jay and his friends are pictorially located in the physical surroundings of the library, the university and a nearby beach, and users are invited to follow him virtually through his quest to find the items on his reading list. The screen tutorial, on the other hand, is all text, with an instruction window linked to animated reproductions of various screens encountered during, for example, a keyword search. Despite the contrast, there is no indication that users find the conjunction of visual and textual literacy demands incompatible or discomforting. While the intention of the developers was that once a user has followed Jay's story and learned how to perform the various functions they see him performing, they will have been inducted into the text world of the library and the visual element will become redundant, in practice the two modes continue to be used together. According to one of the developers, many students continue to access the formal library functions through the informal interface even when they are quite capable of going directly into the library website itself (Cathy Kell, personal communication, February 2007).

In the face of a deeply entrenched preserve of writing, itself a technological practice as many theorists have observed, albeit one in which the technology has become transparent, new multimedia systems of communication in the university depend for their adoption on finding a role in support of written literacy, not as an alternative to it. This fact is often not recognized in the e-learning rhetoric and tensions consequently arise between the established, invariably assessment-related, academic writing practices of the old, and the exploratory, but often academically marginal, innovations of the media-savvy new. Without doubt there is cross-fertilization between the old and the new, just as there is elsewhere in university practice, in interdisciplinary studies, for example, or in professional practice, reflective pedagogies and other sites of praxis. However, as academic literacies theorists have shown, to give learners meaningful access to, and control over, hybrid genres, one has to go beyond the operational and cultural dimensions of literacy education and engage them in a reflexive and critical awareness of personal voice and identity as writers (Lillis 1997; Ivanič 1998). These are the kinds of practices that e-learning technologies need to become sites for, if universities are to exploit them for student learning in the new communications order, rather than mere learning management.

Conclusion

This chapter has explored the concept of literacy, in the context of learning with new media and with reference to e-learning practices, that are becoming increasingly common in today's higher education. I have drawn on a conceptualization, well established in the literature of literacy education (Durrent and Green 1998; Lankshear *et al.* 2000), of operational, cultural and critical dimensions of literacy, to argue that the traditional critical/ analytical reading and writing practices of the university are not, contrary to the rhetorics of literacy crisis or of new media literacies, in the process of being revolutionized by a wave of new media competencies and user content belonging to the newly enfranchised digital native generation. This is because of the embeddedness of cultural assumptions and values associated with print literacies, in the social relations of the academy, the professions, and Western societies in general. I have employed a critique of 'new media' literacies and the 'design curriculum' to put forward two key ideas about the metaphor of technologies as sites of educational practice: one is that it is not the technology of a communication practice that constitutes it as social action, rather the kinds of social relationships that its practitioners enter into with each other and with the 'outside' world; the other is that the kinds of social action that characterize formal educational environments are often in an uneasy tension with those that characterize participants' informal and 'everyday' use of the Internet. While the transformational rhetoric of the e-learning radicals may speak to the current preoccupations of digital insiders, it also works to obscure the role of traditional academic practice in the shaping of e-learning in the university, promoting novel but more ephemeral forms of social practice associated with the spread of the Internet. This is resisted by many education professionals, as Lankshear and Knobel can attest, precisely because of the uncertain nature of the social relations it threatens to create. The conventional teacher-led practices of classroom teaching are not instantly remade in the image of new forms of social networking, despite the claims of their most enthusiastic innovators, but instead they reshape the digital practices to serve their own, far more deep-rooted, social purposes. These purposes are embedded throughout the communicative repertoire of the institution and are long-practised means of social control. This is particularly true of universities, where social goals and communication practices are most deeply embroiled, a case in point being the adherence of disciplinary communities to writing as the primary means of creating cultural capital. This adherence continues despite the proliferation of multimedia communication among academics and between teachers and students, and the ongoing penetration of Internet practices into university pedagogical and administrative life.

I have also argued that the deployment of new media environments as sites where conventional practices of university teaching and learning are carried out creates opportunities for critical awareness of the relationship between technologies and literacy practices to be brought to the fore, as these sites of literacy practice overlap with other sites of social communication where conditions of commercialization and 'economies of attention' combine to generate alternative, often anti-educational, discourses. Critical literacy practices involve reflection on the social world itself, and on our participation in its textual practices. In arguing for a literacies approach to e-learning, I am arguing for critical technology literacy to be part of all pedagogy in the university.

4

The 'university', 'academic' and 'digital' literacies in e-learning

Mary R. Lea

In the previous chapter, Robin offered a challenge to what he refers to as the new media literacies theorists. In some senses this chapter returns to a more conventional view of literacies, focusing very specifically on reading and writing within the different configurations of learning in today's university. I examine a specific aspect of the literacies perspective, 'academic literacies', providing an explanation of research and practice in this field with its relevance to e-learning, and exploring what it might mean to claim that communication in online environments should be conceptualized through a literacies lens as a significant site of academic textual production. I will focus on the textual manifestation of e-learning practice, examining a more contested view of what is going on in online learning than that which is generally apparent in the literature to date. In situating this chapter within the institutional contexts of higher education, which have become associated increasingly with the privileging of written text over spoken and visual, I begin to examine how learning in online environments involves engagement in a range of literacy practices, concerned with writing and reading knowledge, meaning-making and identity, but the significance of which as writing is often overlooked. Additionally, this chapter is set against the backdrop of the changing nature of academic practice in higher education, which I explored in Chapter 1, and is leading to increased documentation and emphasis on the production of texts. For example, the new focus of learning in the university that I examined in Chapter 1, privileges permanent texts rather than ephemeral spoken encounters in its recording of student progress and personal development planning. Indeed, we can discern a development in approaches to learning over the years in UK universities from the traditional Oxbridge model of the student speaking his or her essay to a tutor, through face-to-face seminars and essay writing, towards a more pronounced emphasis on codification through texts and formal assessment processes, much of which is dominated by writing, whatever the nature and materiality of its form. Nowadays, even in the most traditional of university settings, lecture notes are frequently uploaded onto departmental websites for students to access at a later stage. Students, too, are increasingly required to provide handouts and even PowerPoint slides for their own seminar presentations. Rather than less writing, there is actually more writing in today's university, and it is perhaps curious that some literacies researchers are turning their attention so firmly towards multimodality when so much writing still predominates, despite the multimodal environment in which it might be embedded (Language and Education 2001).

Broader shifts from mode 1 to mode 2 knowledge production (see Chapter 1) have reconfigured the position of universities, so that they are no longer the sole producers of knowledge, challenging the very status of traditional disciplines and how knowledge is created (Delanty 2001). However, such moves have not resulted in less codification of these new forms of knowledge; the development of new and web-based technologies has resulted in more – rather than less – writing and reading, more diversity and more variety in textual practices. For example, the merging of issues of pedagogy and the management of learning, via the use of VLEs, valorizes writing in its many different forms and manifestations. I argue in this chapter that the theoretical and practice-based framing offered by academic literacies research, with its focus on the examination of texts and their production in institutional contexts, helps us find ways of exploring these changes and their implications for practitioners. Although mode 2 knowledge is produced primarily outside the university, this has resulted in more emphasis upon personal and experiential knowledge in relation to learning. Having been legitimized in workplace settings, this is being drawn back into the university primarily through courses which integrate attention to professional and vocational practice with theory, although increasingly 'traditional' disciplines are also requiring some form of personal reflection from their students (Creme 2000). Central to these shifts in what counts as the production of 'legitimate' knowledge is the integration of reflective writing into assessment (Stierer 2000; Creme 2005; Rai 2006). In addition, developments in terms of personal development planning and e-portfolios are already resulting in new kinds of texts, requiring students to engage with these hybrid genres (see Chapter 6 for further discussion).

Perspectives on collaborative learning

The last quarter of the twentieth century saw both a linguistic turn in the social sciences and a social turn in linguistics (Gee 2000); given this, it is somewhat surprising that – as Robin indicated in Chapter 2 – language has remained backstage in approaches to online learning in post-compulsory education, particularly since as a discipline education has tended to look to the social sciences more broadly for much of its theoretical framing. This is perhaps even more remarkable since social constructivism, which draws on the work of Vygotsky, underlies many of the principles of online learning, and Vygotsky himself was particularly interested in the nature of language as a mediating tool. Although his focus was on child development, he was primarily concerned with the ways in which learning occurs as a result of social interaction, and, in this respect, he saw both artefacts and language as mediating tools with the capacity to shape and transform mental functioning. In school-based contexts, research has drawn substantially on Vygotsky in exploring how pupils can learn together in what is termed the 'zone of proximal development' (ZPD); the ZPD is created within particular learning contexts as learners interact with others in an activity. The idea, which has been taken up enthusiastically in both the primary and secondary classroom, is that by working in collaboration learners can achieve much more than they would, possibly, be able to do on their own. However, research in this area has tended to emphasize spoken language, talk and dialogue, that is, ephemeral encounters (Mercer 1995), and this has also been the case in relation to children's use of computers in the school classroom (Wegerif and Scrimshaw 1997).

We saw in Chapter 2 how ideas of collaboration have proved particularly persuasive for distance educators and e-learning practitioners in higher education, who have foregrounded the potential for students working together collaboratively in electronic spaces. Similar principles were already in vogue in the early 1990s with attention being paid to the value of group work in university settings; although the latter was driven less by the supposed advantages to student learners of collaboration and more often as a method of dealing with large student numbers (Gibbs 1995). Related imperatives are now driving e-learning, and this has resulted in some arguing that large-scale online learning at a distance will result inevitably in a two-tier education system. Brown and Duguid (2000) suggest that those groups of people who have been previously excluded from higher education may be offered virtual access to higher education but this is still likely to leave them marginalized from the full range of resources offered in face-to-face university teaching. Coupled with widening participation agendas, e-learning may be able to provide degree-level study for previously disadvantaged groups, but elite institutions with their physically located faculties are still likely to be regarded as offering a superior experience, with tuition fees to match.

Building on the foundations laid down by Vygotsky's work, the constructivist frame has dominated approaches to learning in online contexts; more specifically, claims are often made for the benefits that can accrue in terms of the learning experience when students are able to engage in online debates with their peers, rather than learning alone. In this respect, it is common to see the conceptualization of students' 'construction of knowledge' being based on social-constructivist principles. In an edited book by Jonassen and Land (2000), claims are made for paradigm shifts in understanding student learning based on constructivism, with a more conversational and social view of learning replacing a transmission model. Nevertheless, despite a focus by contributors on meaning-making as socially negotiated and co-constructed, attention to the ways in which language itself is implicated in such processes is noticeably absent. Even though asynchronous computer conference discussion has generally been the dominant medium for collaborative construction of knowledge work online, exploration of the relationship between knowledge, language form and the genre conventions involved in learning have been remarkably absent. However, during the last decade attention to the approaches offered by social linguistics has provided the basis for some explorations of the nature of language and literacies and their relationship to learning in online contexts. This research foregrounds the textual nature of online interactions, examining the implications of understanding these as contextualized social and cultural literacy practices. For example, researchers have examined the relationship between the writing students do online and the writing they do for their assignments (Lea 2001; Goodfellow *et al.* 2004), the use of hypertext documents as alternative spaces for assessment (McKenna 2006), argumentation online (Coffin and Hewings 2005), the complexity of the rhetorical demands of online discussion and its assessment (Goodfellow and Lea 2005) and developing a critical awareness of writing practices for online learners (Goodfellow 2005b).

Language in education and academic literacies

In drawing research on academic literacies into explorations of online learning, this chapter goes some way towards providing a complementary perspective to the constructivist approaches which underpin collaborative learning and its assessment. This means turning our attention away from the framing offered by social and cultural psychology towards the field of literacies research, which is informed primarily by applied, social and critical linguistics and, methodologically, takes its cues from the ethnographic method and social anthropology; these disciplines offer us valuable theoretical perspectives for exploring the textual nature of online teaching and learning. I suggest that because research into online learning has tended to ignore language in general and, more importantly, has paid little if any attention to viewing language as social practice in online interactions, it has failed to address the social and cultural conditions of text production, which are central to understanding learning and assessment in the university (Lea and Street 1998). In order to redress this balance I turn to a body of research in the tradition of 'language in education' more generally, with particular attention being paid to literacies in the learning process.

'Language in education' is characterized by research in the New Literacy Studies, a field which emerged in the 1980s when questions began to be raised about traditional views of literacy (Halliday 1978; Heath 1983; Street 1984; Cook-Gumperz 1986; Gee 1992; Barton 1994). As Robin discussed in the previous chapter, Street made a major contribution to the development of this field when he made the distinction between what he termed 'autonomous' and 'ideological' models of literacy (Street 1984). He argued that the popular view of literacy is one of a decontextualized skill, that is, the belief that once one has mastered the skill of reading and writing it will be comparatively easy to transfer this skill from context to context. This is what Street calls the 'autonomous' model of literacy: autonomous because it is based on the assumption that becoming literate occurs regardless of the social context within which literate activity – reading and writing – takes place. In contrast, through detailed anthropological, ethnographic research in Iran in the late 1970s, Street examined the contextual and social nature of literacy practices, focusing in particular on the relationships of power and authority which are always implicit in any literacy event, that is, any situation in which reading and writing play a part. Street also drew on the earlier seminal work of Heath (1983) which explored how children from different backgrounds had different expressions of literacy, ways of doing things with texts; because some of these were not valued in school contexts, this resulted in the children who engaged in these practices being regarded as 'illiterate', rather than being recognized as competent in 'non-schooled' literacies. For example, children who had been read bedtime stories by their parents from books were advantaged in the school context with its textbooks and classroom libraries, whereas those children whose story telling had come from their parents' oral tradition were disadvantaged because these kinds of narrative skills were not valued highly in the school setting. Both this early work, and later research by New Literacy Studies researchers, provided evidence that writing and reading practices are deeply social and cultural activities (Barton *et al.* 1994). Familiarity with and understanding these practices comes about in specific social contexts, which are overlaid with ideological complexities, for example, with regard to the different values placed on particular kinds of written texts and who has the power to read and write. Street termed this approach to literacy the 'ideological' model because it took account of the ways in which reading and writing embed often conflicting expectations and understandings of the value placed on particular forms of text. This perspective has implications for how we value texts in different contexts, and since texts are integral to knowledge construction it also has implications for our view of knowledge and how some kinds of knowledge are valued more highly than others. In this book we raise questions about the different forms of knowledge which have been valued traditionally within the academy and how e-learning may be providing us with textual environments which are challenging some long-held assumptions around the status of that knowledge.

New Literacy Studies, then, with its roots in sociolinguistics and linguistic anthropology, conceptualizes reading and writing as contextualized social practices. Until the mid-1990s this body of research was concerned with school-based, community and workplace literacies and paid little, if any, attention to literacies in the university; in short, academic researchers had concentrated on exploring other contexts for research purposes, rather than their own context of teaching and learning. Put another way, they had not taken a critical lens to their own texts or their own practices around reading, writing and giving feedback on students' written work. However, by the mid-1990s a number of researchers looking at issues around student writing were providing evidence for the ways in which language was implicated in mean-ing-making in higher education, as students learnt to negotiate different written genres in assessment tasks. What characterized this emerging body of work was its specific focus on writing as a contextualized social practice (Lea 1994; Lillis 1997; Ivanič 1998; Lea and Street 1998). Research has been car-ried out across diverse learning contexts and countries exploring the ways in which meanings are both negotiated and constructed through the process of writing (Thesen 1994; Jones *et al.* 1999; Lea and Stierer 2000). These have provided evidence that student writing is concerned not merely with the acquisition of a set of discrete cognitive skills but involves engagement in a variety of social practices as students become familiar with – and learn to negotiate – a range of complex discourses and genres as part of their studies and associated assessment. The findings have highlighted the significance of the relationship between writing and learning, arguing that, in the context of higher education, literacies and learning can never be decoupled from one another. A central tenet has also been that writing must always be under-stood within the broader institutional context of its production and that this perspective extends to all the texts produced within the academy, not just student writing (Lea and Street 1999; Lea 2004a). For both students and academic staff, meaning and disciplinary knowledge are constructed through the very act of writing (see the discussion of Bazerman's work in Chapter 1).

Within this research tradition, the term *literacies* is used in the plural in order to highlight diversity and variation in both texts and practices, fore-grounding the negotiated nature of meaning-making in academic reading and writing. This contrasts with the use of *literacy* in the singular, which denotes a unique entity, literacy as a thing, or a skill, something that once learnt can be transferred and applied with ease from context to context. With an initial focus on student writers, researchers in the field have provided evidence for the ways in which different participants in the writing process, students and their teachers, exhibit contrasting expectations and under-standings of what is involved in any writing task (Lea 1994, 1998; Lillis 1997; Ivanič 1998; Ivanič *et al.* 2000). Literacies are diverse, variable and context-dependent, providing researchers in the field with evidence for the import-ance of considering literacies as social practices, manifest in the discourses and genres of a particular institutional context.

Academic literacies research provides us with evidence that writing – in part due to its historical association with assessment in anglophone higher education systems – is integral to the process of learning. It is not merely a transparent mode of representation which carries along content; the act of writing constructs bodies of disciplinary, vocational and professional knowledge in particular kinds of ways (Bazerman 1988; Pardoe 2000; Stierer 2000), and for student writers much of this process of knowledge construc-tion through writing takes place in the assessment arena. When we consider writing in higher education we are talking about more than an individual cognitive skill, or the commonly described surface features of language: grammar, spelling and punctuation. Put another way, writing is not just the vessel through which disciplinary content is communicated; writing constructs disciplines (Bazerman 1988). Bazerman makes the crucial point that writing matters because the different choices we make about what we write result in different meanings; therefore, it is the writing itself which constructs knowledge in the academy in diverse ways depending upon the context. As Berkenkotter and Huckin (1995) also argue, disciplines are being reconstructed continually through constantly emerging disciplinary genres in both new and existing subject areas, which are closely tied to the particular disciplinary practices of groups of academics. The association between these practices and disciplinary texts is so interrelated that they suggest that 'genre knowledge is therefore best conceptualized as a form of situated cognition embedded in disciplinary activities' (Berkenkotter and Huckin 1995: 3). Later in this chapter, I consider the importance of this perspective which sees writing at the centre of academic practice for exploring the texts produced in e-learning encounters. Academic literacies researchers have added further to these debates around writing and the construction of disciplinary knowledge – in its broadest sense, including vocational and professional subject areas – in suggesting that students also construct their own understandings of a discipline through writing assignments and, more recently, through their engagement with each other in online discussion.

Literacies and online learning

Building on the perspectives exemplified above, researchers in the UK have begun to apply similar principles and understanding to researching online learning (Lea 2000, 2001; Goodfellow *et al.* 2001, 2004; Goodfellow 2004a, 2004b; Goodfellow and Lea 2005; McKenna 2006). They argue that we cannot consider online discussion only in terms of social or collaborative interaction; the written texts themselves are evidence of student engagement in a range of literacy practices in the process of disciplinary knowledge construction. Adopting such an approach in earlier work, I drew specifically on data from two courses with very different disciplinary orientations and contrasting approaches towards teaching and learning online (Lea 2000). In the first, an undergraduate Philosophy course, students were using the discussion forum to engage in academic debate and try out the construction of philosophical arguments. Although studying at a distance, students had opportunities to meet once a month for tutorials with their teacher, in addition to online support. The second course was a postgraduate course, for distance educators, delivered entirely online and explicitly based upon constructivist principles, where students were encouraged to discuss course issues online with their peers and the tutor was positioned as a facilitator rather than a teacher. In addition, contribution to online discussion was linked to assessment, with students being awarded up to 10 per cent of their marks for integrating online discussion into their written assignments. The ways in which the contrasting underlying pedagogic principles were operationalized online were evidenced through looking in some detail at the texts surrounding these two courses. This included not only looking at the texts of online message postings but also the guidance given to students in course materials about the significance of their online messages in the broader arena of assessment. In addition, in both courses students were interviewed about their experience of studying online. This approach of juxtaposing different types of textual material as research data is a methodology favoured by academic literacies researchers as a way of capturing the relationship between texts and practices in any learning encounter.

Whereas students in the Philosophy course were encouraged to post messages which explored philosophical concepts with others in their tutor group, there was no actual requirement for them to do so, and neither the quality nor quantity of their messages counted towards their assessment. It was evident from looking at the language of the message postings that students were using their messages to develop their own understanding of the academic content of the course. In keeping with the more traditional role of teacher and knowledge holder, tutor postings tended to take on a more didactic tone, and, in interviews, students indicated that they valued the tutor's contributions more than the messages posted by their peers. In contrast, the postgraduate course for distance educators required students to make message postings and integrated this activity into the assessment system; students were awarded marks for engaging in online discussion. In addition, collaborative online work with peers was privileged over reading disciplinary texts and tutors themselves posted very few messages; in interviews students commented negatively on the lack of online contributions from their tutors in the discussion forums. The written genres of message postings reflected the academic content of the course and its concerns with learning through technologies. These contrasted with the more conventional essayist-type genres evident in the messages posted on the undergraduate Philosophy course. The research highlighted how each course embedded its own academic content and context and the postings reflected different relationships of power and authority between students and tutors. Through examining the texts of online learning it was possible to identify how meaning-making in online message postings reflects broader institutional issues with respect to course design and delivery of the course. In online debates with peers, students rehearse subject positions and explore how they understand particular theoretical, conceptual and practical ideas, but this is always performed within the broader institutional context of course delivery. Engaging with the written language of these interactions and the relationship between the texts and the practices associated with them, we are able to gain a more complete understanding of what is going on in this e-learning context. This aspect is explored more fully in Chapter 5.

As I have indicated, in drawing on the framing offered by New Literacy Studies, academic literacies research has paid particular attention to the ways in which power and authority are implicated in the act of writing. It is never neutral, a mere vessel carrying along content; it always embeds issues around who has the right to write and who determines what can or cannot be written about. This is why literacies researchers conceptualize writing as a site of contestation over meaning. Those who hold most power in any particular context have most control over the meanings which are being made through texts. Put simply, a tutor makes decisions about the status of a student's written work, and, therefore, when it comes to assessment, retains authority over what should be written.

This contrasts markedly with approaches to collaborative learning and its constructivist underpinnings, which tend towards a presentation of these learning environments as benign and more equitable, flattening hierarchies between the different participants in online learning. For example, in the exposition of principles for online teaching, tutors are usually positioned as moderators (Salmon 2000), taking a more personal management role, or as facilitators, taking on a less didactic role than that which has traditionally been the case in both distance learning and face-to-face contexts. The teacher is positioned less as a knowledge holder, the 'sage on the stage', and more as knowledge collaborator, the 'guide on the side'. Indeed, I have argued previously that the central tenet of collaborative learning – the tutor as facilitator – masks the power relationships that are involved in assessment and can create tensions in online environments between the tutor as assessor and authority, as the final arbiter of students' work and the grades awarded for that work, and the tutor as an equal in online debates. In fact, students have reported that they value the teachers' contribution over and above that of their peers because they regard it as more authoritative, and analysis of message postings indicates the ways in which tutors take control of message threads in nuanced ways which confirms their position of authority (Lea 2000). The tendency of research in online learning to separate off tutor and student interaction from the broader institutional context of text production adds to the illusion that online learning environments provide participants with non-hierarchical spaces for collaborative communication. In reality, this ignores three key features of online written communication and also its relationship to assessment. First, the authority of tutor message postings is given additional weight by the permanence of the text which is not apparent in other teaching contexts, such as face-to-face seminars. Second, writing and reading always take on a particular kind of significance and authority, depending in part upon who is writing and to whom; online writing is no exception. Third, while both online discussion and assignment writing may sometimes involve the production of similar kinds of texts, the underlying social practices that they embody are usually quite different, particularly with respect to whether they are being assessed.

Work in the field of academic literacies has provided a methodology for understanding the ways in which meanings are contested between the different participants (tutor and students) in learning contexts, by paying particular attention to the broader social, cultural and institutional frameworks within which meaning is negotiated. This process of meaning-making takes place through the production and maintenance of texts, genres and discourses and their relationship to practices, often around student assessment; students may have a different understanding of an assessment task than their tutor does, and as a result may have difficulties understanding feedback on their work. In such circumstances academic literacies research has not just focused on the individual student learner as a problem but has explored how meanings are understood by the different parties involved in relation to the broader institutional context of learning, also taking account of departmental feedback policies and assessment practices. From this perspective, literacies and learning can only be understood in relation to the physically located institution, with its own discourses and practices which students need to engage with in order to be successful in their studies. In contrast, in terms of e-learning, the configuration of the twin metaphors of timelessness and unbounded space, which are called into play in the design of VLEs, persuasively position e-learning as an activity which takes place without the located or deictic constraints associated with more traditional study. However, there is a counter-argument which has already been introduced in Chapter 3, suggesting that because online courses are generally located within the same institutional contexts and institutional practices, what actually goes on in terms of writing often looks remarkably similar to those practices associated with other curriculum delivery and more conventional study. Indeed, universities often go to great lengths to replicate the more familiar environments of learning in their e-learning portals and particularly with respect to their assessment systems (see Cornford and Pollock 2002). In Chapter 1, I examined the contrasts between student learning, as conceptualized in its historical sense as a process of acculturation for university students into disciplinary and subject practices and discourses, and the more recent use of e-learning environments for the management of learning. These two constructions of learning are now being brought together in interesting ways in the e-portfolio movement which, in using digital formats, blurs the distinction between different kinds of written texts, such as student assignments and records of progress, thus raising questions about the kinds of genres which are expected and how these sit with more familiar forms of assessment in the university. Chapter 6 takes these discussions further.

New texts, new technologies: isn't writing old hat?

Chapter 3 has already examined some of the contributions made to debates around learning and technologies, by the New London Group, and the more recent work by the new media literacies theorists. There is no doubt that the nature of multimodal texts deserves attention in any exploration of the literacies perspective we are proposing as an organizing frame for understanding e-learning. The literature on multimodality adopts a semiotic approach, taking account of visual modes, and contrasts this with a purely linguistic approach, focusing on language alone (Kress and van Leeuwen 2001; Kress 2003b). Until recently literacies research drew almost entirely on the latter, but attention to the broader communicative order more generally means that most researchers in the field now address the multimodal nature of both texts and practices (Snyder 2001; Street 2005; Pahl and Rowsell 2006). I take a similar perspective in this chapter but am somewhat cautious about concentrating on multimodality at the expense of writing and reading practices and the concomitant danger of losing the focus which literacies research has provided. My concern here is that the focus on mode might mask attention to issues of power, authority and meaning-making that research into academic literacies has laid bare. Baynham and Prinsloo (2001) encapsulate the value of what they term the 'discursive politics of knowledge production', arguing that New Literacy Studies asks important questions about 'what counts as knowledge, who is allowed to author it, whose interests does it serve, how and by whom is it contested' (Baynham and Prinsloo 2001: 85). Questions such as these have been central to academic literacies research and are at the heart of the perspective we are proposing in this book, leading us to conclude that power is integral to any literate act within the university whatever the mode or medium of its production. Attention to texts always involves attention to multimodality, it is a central feature of text production; even on the printed page multimodality is always present in terms of layout, the style, weight and size of typeface, headings, margin width, etc. Nevertheless, I argue that at least in the anglophone tradition of higher education which is becoming increasingly dominant globally, both through the use of e-learning and the expansion of UK, US and Australian university campuses and in Far East countries, such as China, writing is still the dominant mode for the production and maintenance of knowledge. Students and academics regularly use email, discussion lists and web resources; download documents in electronic formats; log on to social networking sites, such as MySpace and Facebook; write themselves into blogs and wikis. Despite the formal and informal differences between these genres, what typifies them is not primarily their multimodality but their nature as forms of writing and the social relations and practices around this writing. As in other contexts, these acts of writing and reading are not just neutral ones carried out by individual readers and writers, they are always mediated by particular contexts and embed specific kinds of relationships. Writing online in formal learning contexts is no exception; its production raises fundamental questions, such as: Will it be assessed and if so by whom? Who posts when and where? How are message headings maintained? How do students quote from others? How are tutor postings seen in relation to other posters? Who reads messages? Who lurks? How do people use ideas from online debate in their assessed work? Our recent work in this area, in online student-to-student interaction, suggests that we need to pay due attention to online communication both as academic writing and as a site of knowledge production, where individuals jostle for authority over what counts in any particular context (Goodfellow 2005b; Lea forthcoming).

Our own reliance as academics on print-based interfaces and the flat linear page, has been uppermost in our minds when writing this book. Despite the dominance of written genres in the academic world, issues of multimodality do come into play in terms of design and the ease with which it is possible to move between texts and interfaces. Representing the nature of texts and e-learning and the use of the Web is something which has taxed us, as authors, in producing this book. As writers we have struggled with the limitations of the flat, printed page and the need to describe web pages. One answer to this problem is to use screen shots of web pages, but this is not without its problems since a flat page is unable to indicate the interactivity of hyperlinks and possible ways of reading the text. The only strategy available to us as authors is to provide shots of every page being referred to or attempt to describe each individual page, much as I have done in Chapter 1. However, this leaves me unable to describe adequately the true nature of the text and the linked relationship between different points on the page. In addition, copyright issues legislate against our using screen shots extensively. One way around this might have been to choose to 'publish' the book virtually, but we are of course also informed by our own knowledge of what counts, and that traditional book production is still valued highly in the academic community, with its own assessment and selectivity procedures and processes, such as the UK Research Assessment Exercise.

This tension illustrates a dilemma for researchers who are taking a critical lens to 'digital literacies' (see also the further discussion of Street's critique below). By this term I mean literacies, the texts and practices of which are integrally related to a range of digital technologies, enabling texts produced digitally to be transferred between, and manipulated within, a range of different contexts with ease. That is, the text itself is less tied to context than might be the case with more traditional forms of writing, such as a book. The concept of digital literacies foregrounds the fluidity and re-authoring possibilities of such texts, asking fundamental questions about how authority is both subverted and maintained through these textual practices. A similar argument was raised in Chapter 1 concerning the constant updating of web pages on official sites. Our own practices are still dominated by traditional forms of written text, the authoritative book, the journal article, yet we are also researching and authoring in a digital world where more complex forms of text are also central to academic practice, including of course our own.

Similar issues are raised for practitioners working with students who recognize the power of academic writing but are also attempting to find ways of exploring the use of screen-based multimodal texts, which may be able to offer different kinds of textual negotiation and production for their students. One such example is offered by McKenna (2006) who, drawing on her own teaching practice, suggests that the use of hypertext with students offers a challenge to academic writing, both in terms of its lack of linearity and in offering knowledge-making through the use of colour, image, space, sound and voice. Through these devices, she suggests, students are able to offer something other than linear argument and take on new subject positions that would not be possible in conventional academic writing. However, she recognizes that the possibilities for subversion of traditionally academic conventions may in part be due to the fact that the hypertext documents her students created were located outside the conventional assessment system and, in addition, were not subject to disciplinary norms, as is the case for students who are expected to conform to particular genres in their assignment writing. Nevertheless, the examples she provides from her own context illustrate the possibilities available for students to subvert more conventional written genres when using hypertext and suggest that this multimodal environment offers possibilities which are not available in essay writing. Clearly in some contexts students are being provided with the opportunities to be creative with multimodal texts and to submit these for assessment, but at the time of writing this is, by and large, still in the arena of the experimental in terms of mainstream course assessment. Nevertheless, contexts such as that described by McKenna (2006) could well help us in taking a critical approach to our exploration of the ways in which technologies and texts are integrated in learning contexts, in particular when they are tied to assessment.

Learning and literacies behind the digital façade

Work by Walton (2004) adds usefully to the above debates; she claims that research on multiliteracies has placed too much emphasis on the visual and the multimodal features of what we see on the screen, in what its authors term the 'new communicative order' (Kress 1998; Cope and Kalantzis 1999). She argues that their perspective is based on a lack of understanding of web design, leading them to believe that individuals using the Web are making their own choices about which paths to take in this so-called non-linear world. In reality, Walton (2004: 94) says that 'digital data are always encoded and stored according to schemes and designed in response to particular organizational, communicational, and technical needs and constraints' She goes on to explore how 'web designers' interface with the internal, invisible level of data is different to the final product seen by the users' (Walton 2004: 95). This contrast between the designer and the user view leads her to ask questions about the model of the world, or we might say the institution, which is embedded in web design and whose interests are served by particular design features. She concludes that a literacies perspective requires us to understand not just what we see as users but what is *behind* the screen in 'the domain of programmers and designers who develop the coding schemes and languages and evolve the systems of categorization that we need to communicate on the Web' (Walton 2004: 118). Walton provides persuasive evidence for her perspective and allows us to step back from the simple view of non-linear learning environments, recognizing the institutional constraints and affordances of their design. What this means in practical terms is that students searching the Web during their studies follow links, possibly in the belief that they are controlling their own path as learners in a web-based environment, when in reality the spaces they are likely to visit are predetermined by the design of the site. This is particularly pertinent in discussions concerning the use of learning objects in course design (see below), in which hyperlinks create pathways and associations between one 'object' (or text) and another.

Although providing a very different critique from that provided by Walton, a note of caution concerning the work of the New London Group on multiliteracies was sounded by Street (1996), before the widespread introduction of VLEs. He suggested that we need to exercise caution when associating literacies with a particular mode, for example, the use of the term 'visual literacies' implying the association of particular kinds of texts with a particular mode, thus masking attention to the nature of literacies as local and contextualized. In terms of the issues we are concerned with in this book, with the associations of the word digital with connotations of dislocation, mobility and virtuality, digital literacies can easily appear as if they are in some way separate from the genres and discourses of the institution, whereas in reality they are as much a part of these as any other academic literacies. Maintaining a focus on the written nature of the texts, the significance of textual practices and their production in digital environments is central to digital literacies as the term is being used here. This enables me to argue that, far from writing being superseded (Kress 2001), writing still prevails in e-learning contexts, in part because of its continued dominance in institutional assessment procedures. Kress and Street (2006) also remind us that any theory of literacy as social practice – although concentrating on reading and writing – is always associated with a range of modes. This seems to be particularly pertinent in the case of online learning, where different modes and media are always being brought together in the construction of texts, which combine written and visual elements in their design. It is the very exploration of texts, modes and media which is at the heart of the approach we are proposing in exploring the interrelationship between learning, literacies and technologies. It is precisely because of the historical association of written texts with the legitimation and regulation of power and authority in institutional meaning-making, what is sometimes referred to as their gatekeeping function, that there are good reasons for the focus I place in this chapter on the written texts of online learning. This perspective enables us to explore the ways in which changes in the medium of course delivery are offering alternative spaces for the production of genres and discourses, which are being played out within – rather than separate from – established institutional practices.

The following example illustrates this point more fully. In a new Open University course which introduced e-learning practitioners to using e-portfolios in their practice, a student – a well-qualified teacher in higher education – asked the following question in an online forum:

> I'm sure this is a daft question . . . but do we have to make sure that any work we've written to include in our e-portfolio is properly referenced?

For example, the 1000 word piece for Activity 2.1 – should we be writing it as we would do any other piece of assessed work? Or, should it just be a piece of more informal personal reflection? I know that everything in the e-portfolio should be our own work or have written permission for inclusion – but does that mean all written submissions need references?

This prompted discussion among the tutors teaching the course, in their own conference, to which the students (such as the one asking the question above) did not have access. Opinions varied widely as to what the student should be told about referencing, but, perhaps more interestingly, in the ensuing online debate a number of issues were raised which included:

- assessment and referencing
- a linear progression in online writing from reflection to academic
- reflection 'getting in the way' of thinking
- a need to talk to students to understand how they perceived these issues
- should we be actively developing new writing genre for online work?
- collaborative writing, how is it assessed?
- issues of ownership in blogs/wikis
- who owns what when it comes to using blogs and wikis in written work?
- what does it mean to write collaboratively?
- copying, plagiarism and cheating
- sharing as central to online learning
- institutional constraints of assessment systems in large institutions, not able to deal with or embrace new forms of textual production
- students need private spaces for writing
- ownership of e-portfolio writing
- giving tutor feedback – what genres?
- what should students read; our list or more widely on the Web?
- how does tutor assess if not familiar with other texts?

The issues raised by the tutors teaching the course encapsulate how explorations of writing, including audience, genre, authority, identity and the relationships between them, lie at the heart of most of the perplexing questions of e-learning practice (see Chapter 6 for further discussion of this course). Although the issues raised above relate to a specific course, we predict that other e-learning environments are likely to raise similar, and other related, issues for tutors and students concerning textual production and its assessment. What is particularly pertinent is how much the institution, and the nature of academia more generally, frames the nature of these discussions around 'what counts' despite the fact that the course itself is delivered entirely online and that the actual subject matter of the course itself is 'e-learning'. The concern of the message poster with the appropriate written genre for her e-portfolio, together with the conversation among tutors which follows, is a useful illustration of the ways in which broader institutional practice permeates even the very newest of e-learning activities. In particular, we see a tension developing between wanting to push the envelope in the development of innovative practice and the constraints of the old, being pulled back to the familiar and to the dominance of authoritative knowledge and its artefacts, the texts with which it is associated. This mirrors some of the conclusions already drawn by McKenna (2006) about the constraints of assessment in innovative uses of hypertext.

Virtual 'learning' environments and 'learning' objects

Despite a predominant institutional focus on the written text, elements of the multimodal environment are implicated in VLEs, such as Blackboard, WebCT, First Class and the Open Source software, Moodle. Online learning platforms generally characterize the learning environment by creating a number of nested virtual spaces, which are differentiated by the use of different icons and other visual displays indicating the nature of a particular space. For example, students may be allocated a tutor group which uses a different image from other tutor groups in the same online forum. Within that group students will probably engage in a range of activities and the spaces for responding to these activities are also identified by particular images. In addition, there are likely to be shared spaces, maybe named 'café' or some other name denoting a social space. Other spaces, for example, 'the seminar room', may allow students from different tutor groups on the same course to come together to exchange ideas related to the course content but not specifically with respect to designated activities. There may be chat areas associated with the course and personal blogs and wikis offered by the software design. To take one example, Moodle offers spaces for assignments, chats, choices (where a teacher asks a question and specifies a choice of multiple responses), discussion forums, glossaries, quizzes, lessons (delivering content), resources, possibilities for reusing web-based learning content, wikis (web pages which can be edited by anyone) and workshops. As Figure 4.1 shows, on the Moodle demonstration page, each space is characterized by an integral icon, much as a speech bubble for chats. These choices of forms of representation are interesting for two reasons. First, the iconography is clearly chosen to be instantly recognizable and to make sense to the participants in any online learning context. As such these are images associated with more conventional contexts of higher education but, arguably, images associated primarily with an anglophone tradition, embedding cultural associations around learning and its artefacts. Consequently, even something apparently as innocuous as the choices of symbols and icons embeds our culturally bound understandings of how knowledge is created. In addition, each time a student or tutor makes a decision about the appropriate space for an online posting in one of these spaces, implicit questions are raised about the status and validation of that knowledge (Lea 2000). This reminds us that knowledge creation is never a neutral endeavour, whatever the technologies being brought into play.

Figure 4.1   Moodle demonstration features

A further area for exploration in terms of broader academic practice is the present-day use of reversionable course material in e-learning, primarily through the use of 'learning objects' (see also Chapter 2). These are 'bite-sized' chunks of texts which can be used in one online course and then pulled apart, reordered and reused in a different course or context. Their design is based on a view of texts as context-free, where the meaning resides in the text itself and, therefore, can be easily transferred from one context to another. This perspective shares much in common with the view of language as an empty vessel carrying along content, in that it embeds the assumption that texts can be understood outside of the social or cultural context of their production. As Weller *et al.* (2003: 2) describe it, 'a learning object is a digital piece of learning material that addresses a clearly identifiable topic or learning outcome and has the potential to be reused in different contexts'. Texts are designed to be decoupled from a broader narrative or schema and to stand alone so that they can be used in an infinite range of combinations. Learning in a course designed on the basis of learning objects becomes more a matter of assemblage (Lankshear *et al.* 2002), and less one of progression and engagement in different levels of knowledge complexity, as has been the case conventionally in student learning. Students are encouraged to pick and mix from a range of learning objects, rather than engaging in a linear progression from text to text. This approach to learning design is clearly linked to changes in the nature and status of knowledge and better suited to mode 2 rather than mode 1 knowledge production, thus privileging ways of learning and understanding which are decoupled from academic disciplines and subject bases. Rather than critical engagement with a potentially infinite disciplinary body of knowledge, learning is conceptualized in terms of reordering and reassembling manageable chunks of textual information. Although, in principle, a book could be conceptualized as a learning object, in practice the texts of learning objects are generally short, content-focused, and broken up into manageable chunks. Advocates of learning objects argue that learners never read books in the way the writer intended anyway, and because they are selective in what they read for their own purposes learning objects can do this job for the student, providing short, bite-sized chunks of knowledge (Downes 2001). This design removes the need for any requirement on the part of the student to engage critically with any sustained argument being developed by a single author. Although it may well be true that students (or, for that matter, academics) are selective in their reading, a book is always situated in a broader narrative, and although the student may well be selective in what parts of the book they read they are generally in a position to see the wider picture. In using learning objects, breaking things up into chunks and concentrating on small reusable texts, written and multimodal, learning becomes oriented towards assemblage rather than critical engagement and analysis. The use of learning objects to provide short texts, automatic reminders of work, and tests through the use of quizzes and games, all go to make up a very different kind of learning experience from that traditionally associated with mode 1 knowledge production.

Although both the approaches offered by McKenna and the proponents of learning objects challenge the dominance of the conventional academic text, and the experiences of both reader and writer, they provide quite marked differences in their approaches to student learning. McKenna provides a space for her students to think outside the conventional written texts of the academy, challenging both subject positions and the sense of audience, exploring the possibilities for text to be endless, with no obvious end-point in the hypertext document for either writer or reader – in essence, providing the possibilities for critique which Robin calls for in Chapter 3. In contrast, although students can make choices about their pathways in a course designed using learning objects, the focus is primarily on processing content which is tied explicitly to course learning outcomes. Most importantly, bits and pieces of content can be taken from one course and inserted into another and tied to a different set of outcomes. The assumption that text is context-free and easily transportable, contrasts markedly with our literacies perspective which views the production of texts as closely tied to the social and cultural practices which are enacted around the reading and writing of that text in a specific context.

Conclusion

Once we acknowledge that writing and reading still count, and indeed are at the heart of how universities function, then paying attention to textual production and associated practices is as important in understanding e-learning as it is any other learning context. E-learning does not sit in a non-textual space just because it is carried out in a virtual environment; it is never decoupled from deeper concerns about how knowledge is made and who has the power and authority over that knowledge. Yet the dominant and often celebratory rhetoric for changing teaching and learning through the implementation of e-learning, and its associated technologies, suggests decontextualized activity, removed from, and therefore unconstrained by, institutional considerations. Simultaneously, though, the tying down of teaching and assessment procedures and policies in association with the development of e-learning is evidence for institutional activity and the restraints it generates.

In both this chapter and the preceding one, we have seen how textual production is always central to the institutional endeavour whatever the technologies involved. As a distance learning institution, the Open University has always been instantiated through its texts, in part because, historically, neither students nor their tutors have been present on the university campus and also because it has provided a form of mass education, the sheer scale of which has required bureaucratic and administrative procedures which have always been codified in text, in ways which have not, to date, been so necessary in face-to-face institutions with smaller student numbers. As I explored in Chapter 1, significant changes in higher education have resulted in all universities finding themselves competing in the global marketplace. In tandem with these developments, the focus on codification and texts has become central to all academic institutional practice. The changing role of the academic, too, is charted through its association with both traditional and new textual artefacts. Evidence for this can be found in terms of the requirement for audit and quality procedures (in the UK) in relation to the Research Assessment Exercise, in which the status of publications and research grant proposals is under continual scrutiny. It is not just students who are being required to account for themselves textually. In both instances, the textual artefacts themselves become what is important rather than the processes they are meant to represent. An example from our own institution centres around the requirement for supervisors to produce twice yearly reports on doctoral students. Of course persuasive arguments can be made for this practice in supporting postgraduate student learning, and indeed it is a requirement of the Department for Education and Skills that supervisory activity is well documented. However, in practice, the completion of the required forms becomes an activity in itself both for the students and the tutors; completing the text becomes the focus of an electronic interaction between student and tutor, rather than the more usual face-to-face relationship evident in their regular supervisory sessions at the university. For both the student and the tutor, completing the form is seen as an inconvenience, an administrative requirement, pretty much unrelated to the supervisory interaction, but from an institutional perspective 'successful supervision' is codified in the act of completing and submitting the appropriate electronic form. The text itself, therefore, takes on a significance of its own as evidence of successful supervision. Understanding how texts such as these – and not just more conventional academic texts – work is central to understanding practice across the university and the way in which knowledge, procedures and practices become digitally codified.

The focus of this chapter has been on the relationship between academic and digital literacies set against the backdrop of institutional practice. I have attempted to draw out some alternative ways of viewing e-learning which I believe can inform general principles of use for practitioners and educational developers who want to underpin their practice with literacies-focused methodologies. In Chapter 5 we will consider what such principles might mean in terms of actual practice through the exploration of a number of case studies.

5

A literacies approach in practice

Robin Goodfellow and Mary R. Lea

Over the previous chapters we have been developing an argument to challenge policies and pedagogies that focus predominantly on learning technologies as tools (for learning and learning management), and on learners as autonomous, self-managing users and skill-acquirers. This essentially technical-rationalist approach (a term used by Schön 1983 which highlights an underlying faith in the benevolence of the technology) has developed in response to social agendas, such as widening participation, and commercial imperatives, such as the global education 'market'. It blurs traditional boundaries between university life and other aspects of lifelong learning, and between modes of knowledge production conventionally thought to distinguish between academic and market-oriented domains (see the discussion in Chapter 1). In response to this blurring, we take the view that there is a need to critically assess the pedagogies of university teaching in technologized environments. The particular challenge we pose is to develop an approach to e-learning that focuses less on the generic practices of learners as skilled users of technology for study and recreational purposes, and more on the highly contextualized social meanings that are being created by students and teachers in institutional sites of pedagogical activity that are increasingly technology-intensive. In order to understand and engage with these meanings and their processes of production it is necessary to examine the texts and literacy practices through which the many sites of teaching and learning in the university are constructed. This is, in essence, what we mean by a 'literacies perspective'.

In this chapter we first provide an illustration of the rationalist and skills-focused perspective in practice, in the context of what has come to be termed 'information literacy'. We critique this viewpoint by contrasting it with three examples of approaches to teaching that are informed by a social literacies perspective. We then go on to present detailed accounts of two teaching contexts in which a similar social literacies perspective has been applied to pedagogy in the specific curriculum areas of teacher education and biosystems engineering. The aim of presenting these two detailed cases is to illustrate the general principles of a literacies perspective in action in contrasting pedagogical contexts, in support of the claim that this is a challenge for e-learning across the board, not only for areas where there is already a formal interest in text or language. The courses we refer to here are all university courses that were current at the time of writing. They reflect a range of subjects, levels, professional/academic epistemologies, and use of technologies, and are drawn from institutions across the anglophone academic world. At the end of the chapter we consider the implications for promoting the kind of approaches that they exemplify, for educational development across the higher education sector.

Approaches to information literacy

One significant aspect of the increasing use of ICTs in teaching and learning in higher education has been an increased focus on what is termed 'information literacy'. This has developed not only as a pedagogical response, but also as a political one, as information literacy has been presented as an important dimension in the realization of lifelong learning, a key policy of the UK government since the 1990s (see, for example, Department for Education and Employment 1998). The following quote, which comes from a discussion paper produced by the British Educational Communications and Technology Agency (BECTA 2001: 2) illustrates the way that ICT skills have been constructed in terms of literacy and social advantage and disadvantage:

> The proliferation of ICT in education and the expansion of Internet-based information and services further amplify the chasm between the information 'haves' and 'have nots'. . . . Changes in education are likely to mean that ICT skills will become the 'indispensable grammar of modern life' and a 'tool for lifelong learning' . . . Social inclusion and economic development in the 'Information Age' are mutually reinforcing, and for people in low income neighbourhoods, gaining and exploiting ICT skills lead to opportunities to participate fully in local and national economies.

Although the notion of information literacy skills refers to the ability to manage information found in any format, not just that stored electronically, it is frequently linked with discussions around e-learning because the Web has made primary sources more easily accessible, both for students working independently and for teachers and course developers designing activities for use in classroom or VLE contexts. 'Web search' activities, in which students are required to find and explore websites relating to specific topics, are to be found in courses at all levels and right across the curriculum, from Art History to Technology (see, for example, Richmond University's web-based projects website at http://oncampus.richmond.edu/academics/education/projects, accessed March 2007). The information literacy skills that are the justification for activities of this type are generally regarded as those concerned with evaluating, navigating, manipulating and presenting information. These 'skills' are often linked to an emphasis on other key concepts in today's higher education policy agendas, such as 'graduateness' and 'transferable skills', as well as lifelong learning. It is argued that in terms of employability and the knowledge economy it is increasingly important to equip students with information literacy skills so that they are able to access and manage information effectively both as a student and in the workplace.

We can illustrate this institutional view of information literacy by looking at the way our own institution goes about supporting the curriculum when learning is often online and always at a distance. The UK Open University has more than 150,000 undergraduate students studying worldwide. All of these students have online access to the OU Library where they are able to access a wide variety of materials and resources, both specifically in relation to their course and more broadly for general information which they might find of interest. The OU Library has been charged with supporting the key skill for students of information handling, which the university's learning and teaching strategy sees as preparing students for the knowledge society. The OU Library's information skills advice for course developers highlights four points concerning information literacy:

1. Information literacy skills incorporate knowledge about where information comes from and information sources, as well as evaluating, navigating, manipulating and presenting information.
2. Information literacy is about critical thinking – on the surface technology, and in particular the Internet, makes information more accessible but it is important to ensure that our students become critical consumers of information.
3. Information literacy skills are distinct from IT skills. IT skills enable the student to use the tools and systems which provide access to information; information literacy skills enable the user to make sense of the information they find.
4. Information literacy skills refer to information found in any format, not just that stored electronically.

As guidance for course developers, the following are suggested as basic learning outcomes for courses which will address information literacy:

- identify a need for information on a topic
- be aware of key information resources and systems in a subject area
- plan and carry out a search for information on a topic using the most appropriate sources
- critically evaluate information
- organizing information so that it can be retrieved and presented.

Course teams are advised to develop activities which develop students' skills in information literacy which include: using a library; locating and evaluating journals; finding and commenting on an academic article; using the Web; finding topical information; and, finding technical data. Students are also encouraged to access a library website which provides access to selected quality-assessed Internet resources for OU courses. These resources are selected by course teams and the library's information specialists. In addition to this course-specific resource, students can also access a resource called SAFARI (Skills in Accessing, Finding and Reviewing Information). These pages are designed to help students recognize what information they need, find that information, evaluate its quality and use it effectively, described on the site as 'all important information skills'. Students can also get advice on 'organizing information using references and bibliographies' and can work through in detail issues involved in evaluation of sources, information quality, relevance, presentation, objectivity, method, provenance and timeliness.

The OU Library's sites are well designed and well organized and there is no doubt that they provide students with a valuable online resource in supporting their study. Indeed, the OU is recognized worldwide as offering comprehensive support for learners studying at a distance. Our interest here is in the *implicit* models of knowledge that underpin the notion of information literacy, as it is instantiated in these web resources. The focus is primarily on information as a thing, something that – given the right tools and appropriate technologies – is accessible, transportable, usable and able to be evaluated. Despite the references to critical thinking, students are positioned as passive consumers and readers of information. This resonates with 'study skills' models of learning in higher education more broadly, that is, with the right training students will be able to master the skills required to become 'informationally literate', a transferable skill for life, as useful in the university as in the workplace.

Looking through our literacies lens, we examine below three vignettes which broaden the boundaries of our understanding of the field. The first of these is a project on Web and information literacy at the University of Cape Town. The second is a course on digital literacy, at a UK university, and the last is a report on some of our own work in the Open University on discussions around plagiarism. These three vignettes offer a different perspective on information literacy from that discussed above, foregrounding the part that understanding and interrogating information plays in the negotiation of, and participation in, knowledge creation and the recognition of the partial and contested nature of what counts as information in different contexts.

Web literacy in a South African context

We begin by considering a critical action research project carried out at the University of Cape Town. Full details of this project can be found in Walton and Archer (2004). The authors discuss the Web literacy section of an academic literacy course, Introduction to Communication, for first-year engineering students. The course integrates a focus on sustainable rural development with teaching communication skills. In order to provide scaffolding in Web searching, the course is studied online by students in a computer lab. Walton and Archer (2004: 177) suggest that this scaffolding is able to make 'tasks meaningful by building on and recruiting what learners already know'. In so doing they provide an alternative perspective to the view of learners as initially deficient in information, as implied by the BECTA quote above – a view which underpins 'skills' models of literacy more generally. They suggest that, for their students, problems with what they term 'web literacy' reflect a more general difficulty arising from educational disadvantage and limited exposure to academic systems of interpretation and beliefs about knowledge. The students who participated in the course came from a 'resource-impoverished' environment, having varied levels of access to cultural resources, such as newspapers, books, letters and computers. Most had English as a second language. Despite their limited experience of using computers, once they were at UCT they quickly developed general computer skills and became adept at using them for personal email and text messaging. Against this backdrop, the project set out to find out more about students' information-seeking practices and also about the researchers' own practices as online teachers, motivated by the belief that this increased understanding would help the authors develop a scaffolded curriculum for learning.

Based on their observations and interviews with students about their web searching practices, Walton and Archer (2004: 179) suggest that in order to be able to undertake a critical evaluation of web resources, students already have to be in command of 'domain-specific academic discourses'. Teaching technical web searching skills is of little value if students are not already familiar with the specific subject discourse and vocabulary, and it can result in conscientious and successful students spending time in unproductive searching. Furthermore, students' cultural perceptions of the site's audience and motives were crucial to their understanding of the information it provided (Walton and Archer 2004: 182). One site which students were asked to evaluate as part of their course was chosen because it provided wide-ranging information about rural development projects. The authors report that students often relied on their personal background knowledge of the relationship between a funder and a non-governmental organization rather than applying what the authors call abstract critical thinking skills to their assessment of claims made on the websites. Although participation in the course, and in particular online dialogue around evaluating websites with fellow students, appeared to raise student awareness, the authors still conclude that 'their limited domain knowledge and poor academic literacy set the ceiling for their evaluative insights' (Walton and Archer 2004: 182). Walton and Archer believe that at the start of the project, as teachers, they did not pay enough attention to domain knowledge in supporting students in developing their evaluative frameworks; students' prior frameworks, for example, their own local knowledge of a rural setting, proved to be remarkably resistant to new knowledge and other criteria for evaluation. One student, for example, having been asked to prepare a list of sources of renewable energy, focused entirely on solar technologies because this particular technology was endorsed by a group of rural members whose photograph appeared on the website she was being asked to evaluate. According to the authors, the authority she was bringing to bear on the task was the 'more familiar trusted authority' of the rural community members she had grown up with, rather than the academic criteria that were the focus of the course (Walton and Archer 2004: 183).

These snapshots remind us of the importance of paying particular attention to the knowledge and experience students bring to their evaluation of web resources. As Walton and Archer (2004: 184) argue:

> The formulation of searches, the interpretation of results and the evaluation of web sources are all competencies that require advanced knowledge of academic literacy practices ... these practices can be made visible and carefully mediated to students ... the development of domain-specific academic discourse is integral to developing academic literacy.

The focus of this literacies approach to teaching of information literacy is on the students' background and prior experience, what counts as knowledge in the particular subject domain and familiarizing students with the academic practices of that subject area, thus equipping them with the tools to evaluate web resources through the lens of that particular domain.

Electronic literacy in a UK context

The second vignette looks at the design of a very different environment altogether. 'Communicating in a Digital Age: Theoretical and Practical Issues in Electronic Literacy' was a course offered to undergraduate students at University College London. It was offered in part as a response to an institutional requirement for training in electronic literacy and computer skills, in line with the university's learning and teaching strategy. The course developers used this initiative to offer an accredited half course unit based on a framework which considered issues of electronic literacy through the lens of literacy as contextualized social practice, in contrast to a more skills-based approach. Building on the affordances offered by the Web, hypertext authoring, and synchronous and asynchronous text-based discussion, the team used the course to examine what happens when online modes of academic inquiry and new forms of writing are introduced into the higher education curriculum. Although the course was offered as an accredited free unit to all undergraduates, uptake was mostly among science and technology students rather than students from the humanities or the social sciences, partly because teaching staff in those areas were more likely to see it as an opportunity for students to develop ICT skills and encourage them to enrol. However, rather than focusing on electronic literacy as acquiring competence in a set of discrete technologically focused skills, this course paid particular attention to what it means for students to read, write and create knowledge in electronic environments. These themes were developed over ten weekly sessions:

1. What do we mean by electronic literacy? Writing as technology.
2. Reading, writing and knowledge creation in electronic environments.
3. Writing in hypertext I: a new textuality.
4. Electronic writing communities.
5. On the Internet, nobody knows you're a dog: issues in online identity.
6. Writing in hypertext II: issues of audience, authorial identity, multimedia and print.
7. Language, culture and difference on the Internet.
8. Electronic literacy and society: exploring issues of democracy and power on the Web.
9. Electronic publishing.
10. Speculations on the future and review.

As with the information literacy initiatives we have discussed above, this course included workshops on critiquing and evaluating websites, but in this case students were also learning how to link reading to design, including not only negotiating external websites but also creating their own websites and hypertext documents. In this process they were encouraged to explore issues, such as how it is possible to present knowledge and understanding in a critical way in a hypertext document, and how the integration of visual and textual modes functions in the creation of meaning. The course also explicitly raised questions about what distinguishes such texts from more traditional written forms, and how argument can be developed in hypertext environments as opposed to the conventional academic essay. The course developers have subsequently used their experience on this course to further explore a number of theoretical questions about the type of writing that is taking place in online academic environments, and its relationship to other forms of undergraduate writing.

This approach to electronic literacy offered students the opportunity to examine the ways in which electronic spaces offer different ways of working with information in knowledge-making. In thinking about knowledge-making rather than information-handling, it was possible to explore the Web taking a critical analytic approach to issues, such as democracy and power, audience and authorial identity. Students on this course were not merely information evaluators, they were actively involved in making use of colour, image, sound and voice, and engaging in alternative approaches to knowledge-making in developing their own hypertext documents for end-of-course assessment (McKenna 2006).

Academic literacies in an online context

Our final vignette reports upon our own work on a website we developed as a resource for postgraduate students studying on the Open University's MA in Online and Distance Education (MAODE), a predominantly online and wholly distance learning programme. As with the previous vignette, our approach was not specifically to address information literacy skills. Nevertheless, the online environment of the course design and delivery meant that any attention to knowledge-making was also implicitly about evaluating and using 'information' accessed electronically. Although students were asked to complete conventional assignments for assessment, the greater part of student study involved web-based activity, including searching and evaluating websites, downloading documents and following links in relation to their studies. Against this background, we developed the eWrite Site, an online resource primarily designed to support students in the kinds of communication practices that were involved in studying entirely online within our MA programme. The site consisted of about 50 screen pages of first-person accounts, quizzes, examples of feedback on essays, audio files, activities, references and links to published work on academic writing issues and external sites on similar topics. The eWrite Site attempted to focus on the 'student's eye view' of writing issues (see Goodfellow 2005b for a full description of the resource and a discussion of an action research project focusing on students' take-up of 'critical' stances towards the electronic communication practices of this programme). In addition, a more conventional section on academic writing flagged the multiplicity of styles and audiences which constituted the rhetorical context of these courses. Discussion pages introduced students to the rhetorical complexity which they were required to engage with as they integrated resources from websites, conventional print materials, online discussions with other students and responses to collaborative online activity.

One corollary of engaging with the notion of information literacy through the more exploratory and contested lens evident in the approaches we have considered so far, is that we begin to examine how students take source material and use it in their own work. This leads us inevitably to discussions around plagiarism. We decided to use the eWrite Site to facilitate one such discussion. Although not always specifically mentioned under the banner of information literacy, attention to the use of sources and referencing is often implicit in the information skills approach. The complexity of academic referencing practice and the sensitivity of universities to Internet-based plagiarism have combined to create a climate in which teaching the 'skills' of citation is neither straightforward nor sufficient to prevent students from occasionally coming under suspicion. All students on our MA programme are provided with both course-specific and general university printed guidance on plagiarism. Our concern was that since they are asked to integrate a mix of digital resources in their assessed work on this MA programme, including written text, visuals, web resources and online discussions, the general guidance they received did not adequately address the issue of integrating this mix of resources into their assignments in a legitimate manner. In response, we incorporated into the eWrite Site an online resource ('Academic Writing and TMAs[1] – Conversation about Plagiarism') based on

---

[1] Tutor-marked assignments.

an audio dialogue between the two of us about plagiarism and referencing, specifically in the context of our own programme with its particular requirements for assessment. With this resource students were able to listen to audio files of our discussion around plagiarism and at the same time access the sample texts on the screen that we were discussing and open 'pop-ups' where there were questions raised in our conversations around referencing conventions (Figure 5.1). We introduced the topic of plagiarism by pointing to the conventions laid out in the course assignment guides and the more general university advice and guidance on plagiarism, but noted that although these provided useful overviews, the examples for using resources did not really address the kinds of things students on the MAODE had to do as part of their involvement in the construction of knowledge using electronic texts. For example, in terms of referencing electronic sources, they were required to cite and make proper reference to not only sources from public web pages but also the words of their peers in online messages and the texts in the course electronic study guides.

We focused our audio dialogue around three versions of a text that a student might submit for assessment, illustrating contrasting uses of referencing and the consequences for the issue of plagiarism (Figure 5.1 illustrates one of these versions, student example A). In particular, we paid attention in our discussions to the need to reference all source material wherever it had come from. For example, we foregrounded issues around citing the words of others from online discussions, referencing online books and course guides and the fact that even though web resources were usually not exposed to academic peer review procedures, in the same way as published works, the issues of ownership of academic ideas still pertain. Figure 5.1 shows a pop-up window containing text from an online discussion that the student has used in the assignment without referencing. This alerts students to the ways that they are expected to reference the words of others

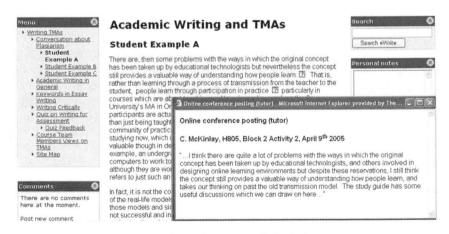

Figure 5.1   The eWrite Site – discussions around plagiarism

on this course – in this particular instance paying due attention to the author of the words the student has used in the assignment, even though those words only appeared in online debate rather than in a more conventional academic text. This approach foregrounded not just the accessing and evaluation of a range of different Web resources but the need to take this forward in completing assignments, in particular providing the opportunity to explore how students drew on resources in their own construction of knowledge. The multimodality offered by the eWrite Site provided us with the opportunity to explore these issues through different lenses simultaneously.

All three of these vignettes take a view of the 'information' in information literacy as always contested, linking it closely to views of students' own interpretation of knowledge, what counts as knowledge and who has the power over knowledge, and giving a sense of agency to students as active participants in knowledge-making rather than as 'consumers of information'. The emphasis is not on information as a downloadable, usable resource able to be navigated, presented, manipulated and evaluated, but on what it means to draw on resources in the critical and active engagement in meaning-making. Each vignette reports upon a very different context with very different groups of students studying at different levels; what unifies them is an underlying notion of literacy as contextualized social practice.

Case studies of literacies-based pedagogy

In the following two sections we present two in-depth studies of literacies-based approaches to teaching with technology. One is a study of reflective writing using a weblog, on a Postgraduate Certificate in Education (PGCE) course at the University of Wolverhampton in the UK. The other is a study of role-playing in a multimedia document environment, at Iowa State University in the USA. The practitioners who have developed these approaches might not themselves label them as literacies-based, or might use other theoretical understandings to frame their practice, but we present their work as examples of a literacies approach with their approval. They exhibit the same kind of focus on meaning-making as social practice that we have been describing throughout the book, and they are concerned with the use of technology as a site in which this practice can be developed and critiqued. They are also evidently successful examples of e-learning pedagogies which foreground textual communication against a background of the multiple modalities of the electronic media. We examine each case for its justification for using its technologies, that is, how it extends or enhances the quality of teaching, rather than simply making the management of learning easier; for its relevance to the needs of its specific subject and practice area, rather than as an attempt to provide a universal learning or teaching solution; and for its foregrounding of the texts and literacies that construct both the university learning context and the domain of professional practice to which the students aspire.

Case study one: reflective writing practices in postgraduate teacher education

The focus of this study is the reflective writing practices of a group of students and their teacher on a postgraduate teacher education course, a focus which reflects the educational philosophy of the course itself and the social literacies approach of this particular teacher. The case describes the way that this philosophy and pedagogy were realized by the teacher and students within an environment that included weblogs and other sites of electronic text construction within the university e-portfolio system. This approach is in some ways itself a challenge to established non-e-learning practices in the teacher education field in general. The case shows how the approach interacts with more conventional practices of teacher education courses, and in the process both reshapes and gives new meaning to them for the participants.

Background to the PGCE at Wolverhampton University

Wolverhampton's PGCE had approximately 100 full-time students in 2005–6, studying to qualify as teachers in further education. The cohort was divided into eight groups, each with a personal tutor. Most of the teaching was done in face-to-face groups, supported by the University's VLE which is used by the majority of Wolverhampton's courses, and a separate e-portfolio system called PebblePad which is used by a few. One of the modules of the PGCE, Developing Reflective Practice, was considered by Julie Hughes (lecturer in education at Wolverhampton and leader for this module) to be particularly appropriate for the use of PebblePad, and she herself made extensive use of it with her own tutor group, who are the focus of this study. The information for the study comes from face-to-face interviews with her and her students and from Hughes' own writing (Hughes and Edwards 2005) and website describing her work.

Hughes's approach to teaching on the Developing Reflective Practice module is very much in accordance with the longstanding commitment that teacher education for the post-compulsory sector, in the UK, has had to promoting and embedding reflective practice. Driven by UK government standards, the sector has promoted reflection and action planning through the creation of portfolios that evidence professional development. With the more recent development of interest in e-portfolios, teacher education practitioners, such as Hughes, have found themselves with the opportunity to enhance their approach to reflective writing through the use of electronic media, but in doing so they have also found themselves at odds with established approaches to reflection on teacher education programmes, in which reflective writing, constructed as solitary activity, is submitted for summative assessment at the end of a module. For Hughes, the availability of the University's e-portfolio platform was the opportunity to develop a more dialogic approach to developing reflection and reflective writing in new teachers. In recognition of Bolton's (2005) characterization of professional reflective practice as a messy and complex political and social activity, Hughes's approach to using the e-portfolio software was to focus on communal and creative aspects of the practice rather than on individual, normative and assessment-related dimensions.

Assessment on the PGCE

The course, and the reflective practice module, covered two semesters, beginning with a two-week induction for the whole cohort, which Hughes led. In this induction all the students were introduced to the requirement to maintain a personal portfolio of practice that was central to the course and to its assessment. The form of this portfolio was a matter for themselves and their personal tutor, the assessor. The principal options were to do it on paper, using university-provided folders and templates, or to do it electronically, using the e-portfolio system. All the students were introduced to the e-portfolio environment, and encouraged to create a personal blog which could be used for an initial 'learning autobiography' and which might become the basis for the learning journal they were required to keep throughout the course, and which would also form part of the eventual assessment. Following the induction, the schedule for both semesters was divided into: two days per week placement in a further education college, where the students were supported by college-based teacher/mentors; five hours per week classes at the University, with the various module tutors; and two and half hours per week tutorials and portfolio development with the personal tutor group. One month of each semester was also spent in individual activity, such as teaching preparation, classroom observation, revision and advance reading.

Hughes's tutor group were the only students on the PGCE course who used the e-portfolio system for their reflective writing work and the creation of their practice portfolios. This directly reflected her own encouragement and support for them in doing so, and the absence of any similar encouragement from tutors from the other groups. One other tutor created a blog for their tutorial group, but otherwise all other students did their reflective writing on paper and compiled a paper-based portfolio. The reluctance of the other tutors to use the e-portfolio system may have been due in part to their awareness of the technical problems that had arisen with the system during its piloting phase in the previous year, but Hughes was also of the opinion that the designed purpose of the system – to promote creativity and imagination in students' writing and other work, rather than simply to support personal development planning, progress reporting, etc. – was one that challenged embedded practice on the course. Her approach was to use the e-portfolio for the development of 'stories of learning', which was in contrast to the tutorial processes associated with the more conventional written assignments and the assessment of individual reflective writing practised on the other modules of the course. Hughes wished to emphasize 'talkback', as she termed it, as a key element in the building of these stories, and the development of relationships between herself and the students and among the students themselves. Talkback involves readers in responding to written reflection in kind, and Hughes sought to maximize it within her group by getting as many people as possible into the e-portfolio environment, where they could interact in writing more spontaneously than they could do on paper. In contrast, in the other modules, which focused upon activities, such as designing an online learning resource, or carrying out a small-scale piece of research, or examining the way that testing and evaluation are linked to theory, assignments tended to take the form of essays or reports. The practice elements, involving other writing tasks and genres, such as lesson plans, observation reports and descriptions of resources, many using structured paper-based templates provided by the university, were assessed as part of the individual's overall portfolio. The reflective writing component consisted of a weekly learning journal and a reflective essay at the end of each semester, both of which were also subject to individual assessment. Other individual assessments were also made for practical teaching, three times during the second semester.

The case

Hughes's tutor group of 12 students was assigned to her at the beginning of the course. Her responsibility to this group was to teach the theory of reflective practice through readings and activities, and guide them through the process and production of the learning journal, the reflective essays, and the portfolio of supervised teaching experience. She was also responsible for assessing this work and for marking the individual portfolios (pass or fail). She began the course by presenting them with an e-portfolio of her own – a collection of texts, images, links to files and resources, etc. which she had assembled and designed for presentation to this audience (Figure 5.2).

This she described as an attempt 'to story the course for them'. It was explicitly designed to grow alongside the course as an ongoing reflection on it, with contributions coming from the students as well as from her. The introduction contained an outline of the key stages of the course, and descriptions and examples of the kinds of writing that would be expected from them: the 'learning autobiography', learning journal, reflective essay,

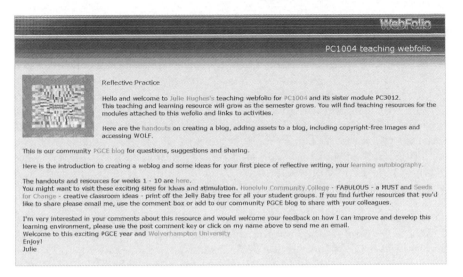

Figure 5.2 Wolverhampton PGCE – Julie Hughes's introduction e-portfolio

lesson plans, etc. It included examples of Hughes's own lesson plans and reflective writing.

The students' first task was to produce a learning autobiography – a story of their career as a learner to date – which they were to share with her. They created these autobiographies in a variety of formats depending on their confidence and inclination. Some used a blog or an e-portfolio page, others produced word-processed documents. Hughes wished to encourage them to be creative and to depart from straightforward descriptive or technical accounts, and it quickly became apparent that this was more likely to happen with personal blogs or other online statements, because the medium enabled them to incorporate images and sound as well as text, and because it supported a dynamic process of talkback and response-to-talkback between her and them. Some of the students, who were less confident about the technical environment, she guided through personalized processes involving initial paper drafts, and then word-processed documents with marginal comments from her serving as a kind of dialogue with the writing. The aim was that they would all eventually begin to work online, in their own time, although not because it was felt that using the e-portfolio system represented a learning outcome in its own right, but rather because it seemed to be the best way to eventually engage them all in a collaborative written dialogue about the nature and purpose of the whole reflective writing activity. The learning autobiographies were succeeded by weekly entries in their online personal learning journals, in which students reflected on experiences in their classes and placement colleges, and also on discussions in face-to-face tutorial sessions around 'critical incidents' from teaching practice. Hughes regularly commented privately on the learning journal entries, seeking to encourage a deeper and more emotionally committed level of individual reflection.

Nine weeks into the course, in one of the face-to-face discussions, people began to express the opinion that it might benefit them to share their written journal entries with each other, as well as talking about their experiences in the tutorials. Hughes encouraged this collaborative development by bringing forward a sharing activity on the metaphors of teaching and learning which she had planned for the second semester. The task was to write 300 words on the topic, 'What metaphors would you choose for learning and teaching?', upload it to their personal blog or other learning journal space and then send a comment with a link to it, to a group discussion area created in the e-portfolio environment. For Hughes, getting the students to understand the resulting online dialogue as *writing* was a key aim of this activity. Many found the process of making written comments on others' contributions initially intimidating, and this had to be eased by explicit discussion of the draft nature of writing in this environment, in which spelling and typing mistakes were tolerated and in which there would be no appraisal of anyone's writing style or ability. Students were encouraged to write directly into the collaborative space without the need for drafting or editing, so as to preserve the spontaneity and creativity of their ideas.

Thereafter, the majority of students contributed regularly to written discussion online. Only one person refused to engage, apparently positioning him/herself as external to the group, perhaps because of having considerably more experience of and knowledge of issues of IT in education than the others. As the single continuous web page that hosted this collaborative discussion grew too big, and the nature of some of the interaction became blurred between reflective comment and social chat, Hughes created a new shared blog which was open to the whole group, and began to encourage people to do their weekly reflections in this public arena instead of in their personal spaces. If they contributed to this it counted as part of their learning journal for assessment purposes, and could be linked to in their portfolios of practice. The collective discussion, thus, became a resource for the development of the personal portfolios that were compiled throughout the course, and a stimulus for the reflective essays that they were required to submit at the end of each semester. All Hughes's group eventually submitted some part of their portfolio for assessment electronically, sometimes with paper-based or scanned-in supplementary evidence, such as written observations made while on placement. Four students also presented assignments done for one of the other modules within their e-portfolios. Another presented a blog which she had developed as a weekly repository, scanning in feedback on microteaching, images (timetables, photos) and other assets she needed to evidence her learning. Some developed within their e-portfolios 'digital stories of learning' (see Barrett 2004) – a direction in which they were encouraged by Hughes, as it involved the optimization of their creative use of media. Two of these students later presented their work at internal and external conferences on e-portfolios in partnership with her. The final assessed reflective essay asked the students to consider and present the theoretical underpinnings of their practice. The variety of approaches to the presentation of written work that characterized the learning journals, e-portfolios and digital stories, also influenced this assignment, so that where students in other groups were producing relatively conventional essay-type assignments, many of Hughes's students opted to use their e-portfolios, with many links to collaborative discussion, to summarize what they had learned about reflection.

The student perspective

In a focus group discussion about the experience of this course, the six students who were interviewed agreed that the written exchanges they had engaged in, in the e-portfolio environment, had been key to the group relationship they had created, which in turn was central to their experience of the course. These exchanges had been characterized by interactivity – speed, responsiveness, spontaneity and humour. Engagement had been further enhanced by the flexibility of being able to contribute from home at any time of the day or night. They felt that this had helped them both to be reflective about their own practice and to understand some of the theorizing about reflective practice that was in the course content. Some were of the opinion that the other (non-e-portfolio) groups had not got as close to each other, nor had produced such extensive and interesting learning journals. They reported that other students had been quite dismissive of the reflective practitioner ideal, but that they themselves had now properly experienced it and could see the value of it. Although the overall PGCE workload was high, and the online involvement actually created more work for them, it did not 'feel like work' because the e-portfolio environment enabled them to be themselves and 'speak' in their own voices. While some had been a bit scared of the technical environment when they first encountered it, it had eventually become 'second nature', and some had adapted it to their purposes in a variety of course contexts including personal communications, placement and conference presentations. They believed that they would continue to use it informally during the next stage of their professional development.

Some students considered that the personal, reflective, writing that they had done in the e-portfolio environment had helped them to be more confident when writing in the more conventional academic contexts of other modules with other tutors, but one or two continued to regard that kind of analytic writing as different and difficult, and not amenable to being approached in the same way. Many of them felt that they had produced, in their e-portfolios, something that they could usefully show to outsiders as evidence of their achievement on this course, although only one had attempted to use the system's structured curriculum vitae or personal development templates for such a purpose. They all valued Hughes's contribution to their course experience highly and felt that she had been 'doing to them' the things that they were learning to do to their own students. They felt that with her help they had constructed themselves as a resource that the University could use for mentoring and induction of future cohorts, and they believed that this would be a useful way to ensure that the benefits of Hughes's approach could be sustained even in her absence.

Discussion

While it might appear that the use of the e-portfolio system in this case was primarily about taking advantage of a particular technology for pedagogical purposes, what Hughes's work actually illustrates is the way that texts can be played out in innovative ways in the learning process. For Hughes, the key value of the medium was in the scope for written dialogue that it both provided and encouraged. This 'talkback' plays an important role in her pedagogy, in the development of the students' critical engagement with practice. It was a feature of her pre-e-learning paper-based teaching, when she would comment extensively in the spaces in and around her students' written texts, occasionally to their dismay, as some felt that the mark of a 'good' piece of reflective writing was that it came back with the minimum of evident teacher response (except perhaps for a satisfactory grade!). Hughes's personal mission has always been to persuade such students (and indeed their other teachers) that the true value of reflective writing is to be found in the response that it elicits from others. In the electronic environment, this response can be brought to the fore. The facility to scrawl spontaneously over a text is lost, but there are instead a variety of ways to attach or insert comments (and to emphasize, highlight or otherwise decorate them) and, of course, the text itself is never 'defaced' as it can be easily recovered in its original form.

Electronic text does have scope for creativity in the presentation of written ideas, via the use of graphical and typographical features and intertextual linking, and the flexibility with which text can be processed online is paralleled by fluidity in the interplay of registers, movement between social chat and the authorial voice, for example. For many of these young professional people, text-based communication practices associated with social networking technologies, such as text-messaging, MSN and MySpace, are familiar and unremarkable (see the discussion of these media in Chapter 3). They are not faced with the problems of 'mastering' systems and devices that are so often attendant on the use of university and other institutional networks, but the medium also inflects their attitude to academic writing and to themselves as academic writers, principally through their interpretation of writing online as different from, and easier than, essay writing. As far as their PGCE experience was concerned, they were not wrong in this because of the insistence on formal standards of essay writing that they met elsewhere in the course. For Hughes this was a source of frustration, as she spent a lot of time signaling to them that much of the academic writing required by the other subject modules could be regarded as an extension of the reflective writing they were doing not as a separate and monolithic genre. In this regard, the e-portfolio environment being seen as a distinct and friendly place in which to communicate served to drive a bit of a wedge between this module and the other, more conventionally taught ones. Hughes's own practices, and her reflexive critique of them, are also perceived by the students as different from the ways that other teachers go about promoting them as writers. Those students who saw a categorical difference between their e-portfolio writing practices and the essays they tried to produce for the subject modules were very aware of the inadequacy of their personal styles to procure good marks from their subject teachers. 'It just comes back' was one comment, meaning that the informal reflective voice, with its tolerance for erratic spelling and casual style, is rejected by the more academically rigorous essayist establishment. Hughes's consciousness of the continuing valorization of technically correct writing by many of her colleagues led to occasional anxiety that she might finally be doing her students' prospects no favours through her focus on expression at the expense of technical accuracy. She is aware that she is stretching the boundaries of what counts as writing in the university, and while she has undoubtedly helped to raise students' critical awareness of these issues, she has not yet managed to resolve the contradiction between the kind of communication the medium encourages, and the conventional requirements for academic success within the university.

An important lesson from this study is that we need to go beyond a purely pedagogical, let alone technological, account if we want to understand the nature of the relation between classroom literacy practices and professional practice. Hughes's student who took no part in the exchanges around reflective writing in the e-portfolio system nevertheless passed the course, and there is no reason to believe that he or she did not go on to become a successful teacher in further education. Similarly, students in the other groups, who did not have Hughes as a teacher and did not use the e-portfolio, still passed the course and, presumably, also went on to be successful teachers. Hughes's approach to the PGCE course is only one among many possible approaches, as she acknowledged. Even as course leader, her attempts to get other teaching colleagues to adopt her own practices had to be limited to an insistence on attempts to generate 'talkback' by whatever method they favoured. Her own approach, and the use of the blogging medium, was developed in response to what she regarded as the 'critical realities of an FE teacher's experience'. These realities, she felt, reflect the technical-rationalist agenda that has come to pervade the management of this sector during the reorganizations, rationalizations and casualizations of the post-1992 era in the UK. Under these conditions, teachers are increasingly subject to performance-linked appraisal, where performance is defined in terms of indices of institutional productivity: numbers of students enrolled against numbers achieving qualification, costs of teaching per student unit, institutional success in meeting government-set targets, etc. Hughes felt, from her own experience, that for many new teachers in further

education, survival needs to come first, but also that the eventual development of a critical confidence is crucial, so that oppressive and instru-
mentalist structures would not always be perpetuated. In order to pursue
constructive change, people need to question, and if necessary contest, the
values inscribed in practice. This is what she believed the students in her
tutor group needed to learn, albeit while they worked to pass the course.
The key to questioning, and perhaps challenging, practice in institutional
contexts is the recognition of the underlying power relations that pertain.
These relations are often revealed in apparent contradictions between the
rhetoric and the reality of the social action embedded in the texts that
students and teachers produce. In the case of the Wolverhampton PGCE,
for example, a fundamental contradiction existed between the rationale for
reflective writing and the requirement to submit it for assessment. On the
one hand, the supposed value of personal reflection, and the way that students were encouraged to do it, was that it allowed people to express themselves without fear of appraisal – this permitted them to present a truthful
account of their strengths and weaknesses as teaching practitioners. On the
other hand, they knew that they would eventually be required to submit
these personal accounts for Hughes's evaluation, on which their qualification and future careers ultimately depended. Hughes's response to this
paradox was to try and make it explicit. Drawing her inspiration from theorists (Brookfield 1995; Bolton 2005), whose work was part of the PGCE syllabus, she challenged the students to question her own textual practices as
well as their own. They were, she argued, telling different stories to different audiences.

This case study locates the complex practices of reflection in teacher education within the site of the production and consumption of the texts in
which they are largely embedded. This site includes the e-learning technologies, which are highlighted because they provide additional possibilities for
textual activity, particularly via social and collaborative activity. The students'
awareness of the kinds of texts they are producing and the relation between
these and the texts that are the standard currency in other parts of the course
is shown to be the basis for a critical understanding of wider aspects of the
practice domain they seek to enter. In the study that follows we see the
attempt to bridge classroom and professional literacy practices taken a step
further, through the use of technologies to simulate an entire domain of
discourse.

Case study two: communication in a simulated document environment

The principal developers of the MyCase multimedia document environment, David Fisher (Assistant Professor of Rhetoric and Writing at the University of Arkansas at Little Rock) and David Russell (Professor of Rhetoric at
Iowa State University), both have backgrounds in rhetoric and the teaching

of writing, so there are close parallels between their approach to university teaching and the social literacies perspective that we are proposing in this book. Rhetorical and social literacies viewpoints both focus on social practice, and the embodiment of practices in texts. In this instance, the MyCase work also draws on activity theory (Leont'ev 1981), which views communication technologies as mediational tools, rather than primarily as sites of practice as we have argued (see Chapter 2). Nevertheless, in contrast to some of the pedagogical approaches we have been critiquing in previous chapters, this work is not primarily concerned with the operational dimension of e-learning but with its epistemological substance – the texts and discourses, what we would call the literacies, of classroom and professional practice.

Background to the MyCase approach

This work originated at Iowa State University (ISU), and the University of Arkansas at Little Rock, in the USA, and has been developed by a cross-faculty group of teachers and graduate students from five departments: English; Business; Genetics, Development, and Cell Biology; Agriculture and Biosystems Engineering; and Philosophy. Many teachers in these departments have used problem-based learning approaches based on cases, or simulations of decision-making processes that occur in real world contexts. A case is a collection of documents and roles that relate to a scenario where a decision has to be made by a hypothetical company or organization working in a specific social or technical field, such as the production of genetically modified foodstuffs. Normally, students are asked to role-play the decision-making process, in the course of which they come to understand the issues in question. While Fisher was teaching technical communication courses at ISU, he and Russell instigated collaboration with individual teachers who were already using 'paper' cases of this kind, with the idea of developing case material in an online multimedia environment, creating an archive of multimedia artefacts which could be used to construct cases for problem-based learning in a variety of subject areas. Fisher describes this as 'remediating' the paper-based cases, borrowing the term from Bolter and Grusin (1999), to emphasize both the enhanced immediacy and authenticity that technology can bring to text-based role plays, and the additional level of reflection on the 'real world' activity of the classroom that such apparent authenticity provokes (Fisher 2006). Fisher and Russell regard the motivational effectiveness of case studies and simulations in conventional teaching contexts as proven (Russell 2005), and with the increased scope for 'visuals, video, database-driven information banks and communication tools' afforded by e-learning technologies (Russell 2005: 1). There is a real possibility for the creation of a textual domain in which students could imagine themselves in situations of professional practice despite being outside the actual practice context. With the collaboration of the Department of Agriculture and Biosystems Engineering at ISU, Fisher and Russell developed one particular textual domain based on a fictitious biotechnology company called Omega Molecular.

In this study we examine a course in technical communication that Fisher taught at ISU in 2004 using the Omega Molecular multimedia environment. Much of the information for this case study has come from the MyCase website which contains theoretical and descriptive papers written by the project developers, including Fisher's PhD thesis, in which this particular course is explored in detail (Fisher 2006). The website also has controlled access to the Omega environment itself and to other environments that have subsequently been developed. In addition, further information about the case has been provided by Fisher and Russell themselves, in interviews carried out by telephone and email.

The Omega case

The Omega case arose out of the ongoing relationship between the Agriculture and Biosystems Engineering Department at ISU, and the English Department, around the provision by the latter of service courses in technical communication, focusing on theories, principles and processes of effective oral, written and visual communication in the technical disciplines. All engineering students at ISU are required to take these service courses for their professional development, but the courses themselves had been seen by students and teachers as problematic, as students often did not see the relevance of the courses to their future professional work. Many consulting firms in the US hire students who are fresh from university and provide them with on-the-job training. For this reason students were often reluctant to take courses which they saw as unnecessary. The development of a more motivational approach to professional communication in these technical areas was seen as a priority by the Department, and Fisher and Russell convinced the subject professors and the University that their e-learning-based approach might be the answer. With the help of contacts provided by the departmental subject experts, they constructed an online document environment representing the business-at-hand of an imaginary small biotechnology company called Omega Molecular, which was involved in the production of genetically modified foodstuffs and required to respond to public opinion and the attention of government regulatory agencies.

This document environment was used to create a simulation in which students play the role of technical consultants to Omega, advising the company on their dealings with the public, news media, commercial world and the regulators. The Omega online environment presents an interface (or 'portal') much like the one employees would face when working on their computer within a contemporary knowledge-intensive organization (Figure 5.3). In it they can log in, gain access to the latest organizational happenings, share file spaces, access documents, reference library, organizational calendar, videos of people talking about company issues, and send and

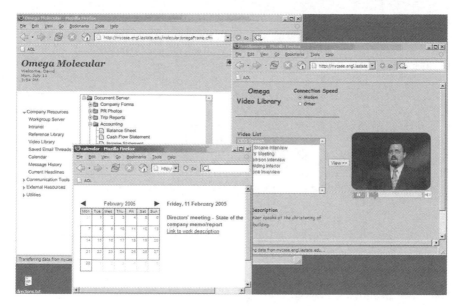

Figure 5.3   MyCase – Omega Molecular portal

receive emails, etc. The environment is designed to immerse students in the sense of working for the company, but it is not an exercise in virtual reality, as Fisher points out: 'there are no avatars or fake buildings. People don't wander around and talk to each other in a virtual world. The environment centers on the texts and what people do with those texts' (personal communication, November 2006). The students' immersion is in the 'complex circulation of discourse among multiple stakeholders who take up and contest multiple disciplinary, ethical and social positions' (Russell 2005: 2).

Figure 5.3 presents one view of the Omega portal, showing in the left background the Company's document server, from which students can download information for their tasks and assignments, and to which they can return the completed assignments; in the right background the interface to video clips of Omega personnel speaking about various issues relating to the tasks and other aspects of Company business; and in the foreground the calendar tool through which work around the assignments is scheduled.

As we have noted, Omega builds on the well established pedagogical approach of getting students to role-play scenarios which simulate the kind of decision-making that professionals might be called on to do in the 'real' (non-classroom) world. Action in this simulated world takes place through the production, distribution, exchange and consumption of writing (Russell 2005), for example, in emails, reports, plans, and websites, that engage students in a discourse-demanding context that appears, relatively convincingly, to draw its rationale from a world of practice outside the classroom. In response to prompts and requests, communicated electronically from virtual characters in the imaginary biotechnology company's management hierarchy (played by the teacher who is leading the course), they are required to produce documented information, opinions and advice relating to the company's policies and practices. For example, in one assignment students view three videos in which the Director of Finance and the Director of Research and Development provide conflicting information about the state of the company. A text-based work order from the Omega chief executive officer then asks students to provide an objective analysis of the company's situation and to make recommendations about its future. The course requires them to work, individually and in groups, on this and a number of other written and oral assignments in which they are expected to produce texts using a variety of media appropriate to specific practice-based formats or genres, such as memos, reports, datasheets, etc. (some examples are shown in Table 5.1).

While these texts and the technologies used to create them help to sustain a convincing illusion of a real company's document environment, the intention of the simulation developers goes beyond a straightforward attempt to replicate business practices for training purposes. The aim of the simulation is to help students 'develop the capacity to speak up, to negotiate, and to be able to engage critically with the conditions of their working lives' (New London Group 1996: 67, quoted in Fisher 2006: 30). As they address the tasks, therefore, students confront a number of more or less contentious issues concerning the way Omega (and companies like it) go about their business, for example:

- Discrepancies between what company officers say in public forums, and the scientific data (or lack thereof) that informs their messages,
- Issues of intellectual property and their relationship to humanitarian and/or for-profit activity,
- The need to assemble a coherent story about the company and its current situation based on information provided in the artifacts and to subsequently adapt that story for various audiences and purposes (e.g. requests for financing for humanitarian projects vs. requests for investment dollars), and
- The continual changing of information available due to events that take place in the 'outside world.'

                                                                    (Fisher 2006: 31)

In addition to their role as part of the simulated practice environment, the tasks also serve as assignments on which students are graded, in the 'real world' context of the ISU technical communication course that the simulation is part of. As in conventional courses, graded assignments are specifically intended to sort and rank the students, as well as to give them the opportunity to display what they have learned individually. But in contrast to conventional academic practice, the Omega assessment process allows students, like employees in many workplace environments, to work in groups and to make use of the work of other students, accessed through a document

Table 5.1 Omega Molecular assignments and genres

Assignment	Text/Task Characteristics	Practice Format/Genre
Define and/or describe a tool/process involved with genetic engineering	(Individual) Incorporation of at least one graphic	Definition for web glossary designed for Omega newcomers
Summarize/synthesize scientific findings	(Group) Using various tables and lab reports provided in the learning environment	State-of-the-company report
Summarize/synthesize financial situation	(Group) Using financial statements and 'testimony' provided in the learning environment	
Create a product/process data sheet	(Individual)	Data sheet for audience interested in learning about/buying process/product; or investor bulletin for venture capitalist interested in investing in the company
Develop and deliver an oral report about political and agricultural conditions in a Southeast Asian country	(Group) Accompanied by PowerPoint presentation	Videotaped presentation to be available on the corporate intranet
Create a proposal or business plan	(Individual)	Proposal directed at funder/business plan directed at potential investor (document criteria available in learning environment)
Develop a public web presence for Omega	(Group) Display and defend in front of class (characterize major argument(s) and how they are rendered in structure and content of site)	Website for the public

sharing system, to develop and refine the work they are submitting for assessment. In fact the sharing process does not even stop at the end of a course, as final documents produced by one student cohort may be used (with the students' permission) by the next course.

Engagement with the Omega case therefore involves students in three parallel, but not always complementary, processes: the 'circulation' of discourse in various media, which means the discussing, producing, commenting on, editing, revising and publishing of multimedia texts in response to the tasks which the simulation sets; reflection on the relevance of those tasks for their future professional and civic life; and the production, submission and grading of texts for assessment and the earning of an individual grade that will ensure them credit for passing the course. Below we describe the way these processes were played out by Fisher and a group of Agricultural Engineering students at ISU on a one-semester technical communication course in 2004. We illustrate the text circulation process as it applied to two of the course assignments (see Table 5.1) in particular: creating a glossary of definitions for Omega newcomers, and creating a data sheet for potential investors.

Omega in practice on a technical communication course at ISU

This course is generally taught to classes of around 25 students in their junior or senior year (the third or fourth year of an undergraduate degree course), many of whom have not taken a writing-intensive course since the first or second year. The 2004 course was conducted in a hybrid distance/face-to-face mode, with the whole class meeting occasionally in a computer classroom or traditional classroom and individual and group work also being carried on remotely by logging into the Omega portal from homes and other campus locations. The students were introduced to the simulation and the Omega portal in an instructional session at the beginning of the course, where they were put into groups and asked to play the role of technical consultants contracted to advise the Omega management. The tasks they were to carry out were initiated through the online calendar (see Figure 5.3), phrased as exigencies within the simulation, that is, something required by one of the Omega key personnel to which the students, as consultants, had to respond. One of the first tasks was to compile a glossary of key terms relating to tools or processes involved in Omega's business of genetic engineering that could be used to help induct new staff into the company. As a class the students decided on the terms that needed to be defined and divided the work of defining them among the groups, so that there would be no redundancy in what was produced. Individuals then researched their allocated terms with the help of model definitions that previous course cohorts had left in a shared area on the document server. The draft glossary entries they produced were uploaded to the same shared area for feedback from the Omega 'management' (role played by Fisher) and to inform further discussion among the groups about the style and format in which the final glossary document would be presented: the degree of institutional standardization, for example, or whether it should be a PDF or a hypertext document.

At the same time as feedback on the first drafts was being received, the task of providing a data sheet for potential investors was initiated from the calendar. This task required the incorporation of some of the specialist terms that were being defined in the glossary, but in the specific context of, for example, providing financial information about the future cost of processes, or providing reassurance about the future viability of technologies with regard to health and safety regulations. These considerations impacted on the students' understandings of the terms they were defining and needed to be integrated into their preparation of the second drafts of the glossary entries. The recycling of work introduced them to the notion of the 'circulation' of texts within an activity system. While a complete cycle from first draft to final revision of a document might be scheduled to take three to four weeks, as the work proceeded more of the tasks began to overlap, and students would eventually be working on up to three at one time, with interrelated feedback at both group and individual stages. Each task had to be worked through at least two drafts, with Fisher commenting on the first draft in the role of the character in the simulation who requested the document, for example, making the kind of edits that a director of marketing or a director of finance might make on a draft. In some cases these comments were highly critical, as Fisher drew on his own experience of the uncompromising way that work is often appraised in business, as opposed to classroom, contexts. For him, the students' appreciation of what it means to write for a corporate audience was an important outcome of this course. These first drafts were not graded, but the feedback from management went into the shared area where other students could see it too.

For many of the students, the idea of not receiving a grade but instead a number of comments in preparation for revision of their documents was something they had never experienced in the school environment, as was the sharing of work in progress with other students. These practices, however, do characterize the workplaces that Omega is simulating, and it is a principle of the approach of Fisher and Russell that the workplace textual forms that the students produce should result from exigencies which accurately simulate those that occur in authentic practice contexts, rather than simply being required by the course. Nevertheless, the production of workplace textual forms is sometimes in conflict with conventional academic practice, for example, in the practice of citing work that has been shared, in order to clearly identify ownership. As Fisher (2006: 69) points out:

> enabling students to draw freely from each other's work as it is posted to a shared file space and from the work published in the [portal] 'without citation', while extremely unusual in classroom settings . . . is much more common in the workplace, where people often draw from a common pool of documents.

For each of the assignments, the first draft was revised on the basis of feedback from the Omega management, and in the light of comments from peers, and classroom discussion of the social motives informing both the students and the Omega hierarchy's perspectives on the task. Where students bought into their roles as consultants in the simulation, the discussions might focus on issues around the company's social responsibilities and its conflicting for-profit and non-profit motivations, even where they resisted the fiction of Omega and focused instead on their real identities as students writing for Fisher, as their teacher, there was still opportunity for reflection both on what it would be like to work for such a company and on the effectiveness of the simulation itself as a vehicle for their development. As Fisher acknowledges, a number of students did resist the role play initially but most were drawn in to discussion about Omega eventually, not least because of the contrast its realism presented to the kinds of unconvincing classroom tasks that these students were used to in their other courses.

The grading system and the need to pass the course were a major part of the social motivation for the students too, of course. To get their grades, they posted the second drafts of their assignment to the document sharing tool, this time for marking by Fisher as teacher. Comments made on this second pass were more teacher-like and aimed at justifying the grade given, which was on a traditional letter scale. Fisher's comments on assignments, at both stages of drafting, and his marking at the second draft stage aimed to reflect the value that a student had added to information that was already available in the portal or shared document area. This value was evident in several ways, for example: through the appropriateness of materials that were selected from the portal for the purpose identified for the document (financial statements for an investor prospectus, rather than detailed scientific data); through presentation of those materials to fit with needs of the audience and the purpose of the organization (providing visuals for positive trends); through the provision of additional information from outside the portal (financial ratios for other organizations in the same industry); through general accuracy and expression. None of the assignments in this course required academic writing competence in the conventional sense, such as involving critical reflection, argument, review and referencing, but Fisher considers that the students on this course do need to develop the capacity to write a long, cohesive document, even though they may never have to create such a document by themselves outside the university. Thus, some of the individual tasks are focused on the production of substantial cohesive texts, such as a business plan, which are themselves conventional genres, albeit not in an academic sense. At the point at which they have to do this, students have become familiar with the portal and with some of the science that underlies the issues affecting the company, so that they are able to use internal and external resources to construct what amounts to an argument in a manner analogous to more conventional academic genres.

The graded assignments were emailed directly back to students who then made any final revisions and placed a clean copy of their work in the portal. Although the grade for the work had already been awarded, they were often motivated to do this by the fact that it would be later viewed by their advisers from the Engineering Department and evaluated in terms of engineering competencies. Each assignment has a component that each student must complete to exhibit a certain level of competence. The extent to which technical competence was implicated, given the central role of media in the course was, however, a matter for negotiation. Again, Fisher believed that as an instructor in technical communication he needed to ensure that students left the class with some idea of how to undertake technical tasks, but, at the same time, he was content for work to get done on a quid-pro-quo basis as it is in professional practice. Thus students with more technical expertise were encouraged to use this to improve the presentation of their group's output, which the better writers might have played a larger role in formulating. By interacting with the groups during the development process, Fisher was able to ensure that individual students engaged with a wider range of competencies. As part of the assessment they were required to identify their contribution to the team effort and to have that identification corroborated by other team-mates. Fisher's close familiarity with the way that the groups worked enabled him to assign an element of the grade for collaboration to individuals that corresponded to both his, and the group's, view of what was merited.

Discussion

This has been a necessarily brief account of a very complex and ambitious teaching design, focusing on a wide range of potential learning outcomes across a number of disciplines. The approach speaks to several of the themes being developed in this book. First, it is an example of an e-learning environment that has been constructed in order to extend and enhance teaching and learning on the courses in which it is employed, and not simply as a more efficient or flexible means of delivery of materials and/or tuition. The approach uses multimedia technologies to create a convincing simulation of a professional 'document environment' with which students can engage as actors. As a simulation-based approach it builds on pedagogical practice which has long been established in paper-based contexts, but it uses technology to give this practice an additional dimension of authenticity which greatly extends the scope for learning activity. Most importantly, however, it does not take either the performance of the technological practices or the production of conventional academic assignments as the key indicators of learning outcomes, but instead rewards student engagement with the professional communication practices it simulates.

Second, it is an example of an e-learning environment developed to support teaching and learning activity in the context of a specific kind of subject matter and pedagogical approach. It is not designed as an 'all-purpose' teaching tool into which it is assumed that the slotting of subject/discipline-specific content and/or the engagement of a variety of pedagogical approaches will be unproblematic. The approach was developed to meet the needs of courses which aim to prepare students to be practitioners in technical fields, such as engineering, agriculture and biotechnology. In the imagined role of technical consultant to a fictitious company whose day-to-day business is represented by a range of online documents, students have the opportunity to experience some of the processes of familiarization with professional practice in a specific context that they will encounter when they move into employment. The approach can therefore be seen as a response to the penetration of mode 2 knowledge production into the university curriculum (which we discussed in Chapter 1) – this relates to professional and/or occupational practices which are displacing some of the more conventional disciplinary content that has previously been the focus of university study. While versions of the MyCase approach have also been used in subject areas which are more aligned to a conventional disciplinary knowledge base, such as genetics, it is the opinion of the developers that the roles available for students to play in these contexts are less accessible because they do not engage them in the same 'document cycling' that the more specifically practice-based ones do.

Third, and most importantly from our point of view, it is an approach to e-learning in which the texts which mediate study activities and the students' engagement with the 'content' of the course are given prominence as forms of social action in their own right. That is, they are not viewed simply as carriers of information about biotechnology or business practice, nor as stimuli to interaction that is intended to promote learning through discussion, reflection, memorization and reformulation, but they are the actual means of getting things done in the simulated domain they construct. The social action performed by the Omega texts *is* embedded in this approach, which is not simply a means to develop ICT, team work or leadership skills, or a prompt to online discussion for its own sake, or a space to interact with others in order to scaffold each others' learning, according to a conventional constructivist e-learning rationale. The texts and technologies are explicitly constructed as a bridge between classroom and workplace, and the fact that some students do get a view across this bridge is evident from their contributions to in-course classroom discussion and their feedback to focus group sessions after the course is finished. In particular, they comment on the difference between writing for Fisher as a teacher, and for him as one of the various Omega personnel who provide the exigencies for the assignments. They even distinguish between these fictitious audiences, noting the different kinds of information required by the company chief executive officer and the marketing director. Their understanding of more abstract dimensions of corporate literacies is developed too, according to Fisher, in their appreciation of the role of standardized presentation formats in constructing institutional 'voice' and corporate identity, or of 'boilerplate' texts that have gone the rounds of approval required from different compliance groups and are no longer amenable to editing by individuals. These social literacy practices are what link the scientific and technological knowledge belonging to the subject areas in which students are seeking to graduate, with the professional domains in which they are hoping eventually to pursue their careers.

Conclusion: implications for educational development

In this chapter we have looked at some examples of courses and pedagogical initiatives in which a literacies perspective is applied, either implicitly or explicitly, to the use of e-learning in higher education. Unfortunately our selection of examples could never be fully representative of relevant practice in higher education, as there are very many e-learning implementations in university courses around the world, and we do not claim to know every one in which literacies play a role. It is probably not coincidental that we ended up with a number of cases from engineering/technology and teacher education, as these are (along with business and computing) areas with significant take-up of learning technologies in general, and they are areas where the convergence of academic and professional knowledges is quite well developed. All our examples are concerned with communication practices in some academic, disciplinary or professional context, but the pedagogical aim is not to master a technology or medium for some generic communicative purpose, but to gain insight into the specific practices and social relations that the technologies are helping to construct, within the context of an academic and professional field to which we assume students aspire to be members. E-learning is not being conceptualized here primarily in terms of the skills and competences it forces students to acquire, nor simply as a means of leveraging individual and collective cognitive problem-solving activity. Rather it is being treated as a site where the academic, disciplinary, social and professional *milieu* of the course is being constructed, and students are being introduced to resources for their own meaning-making and the construction of their own social identity. Pedagogy in these cases focuses on the dialogic nature of texts at both ends of the process, what goes into the lesson as well as what comes out. It focuses too on the kinds of social action that these texts represent, and implicitly on their role in the construction of relations of social power. In these cases teachers are seeking to help learners develop the ability and desire to recognize the kind of knowledge that classroom and other texts construct, to critique the practices and relations they embed, and to realize their own full participation in processes by which both texts and practices are produced and negotiated.

Needless to say, this kind of pedagogical approach is not common in e-learning practice in general. Pedagogies that are explicitly oriented to texts as social practice are by no means widespread, even in the writing and language fields. We have put this down to the dominance in e-learning of what Doherty (2004) calls a 'singular pedagogy' based around the metaphors of discussion and community and rationalized in terms of the social-constructivist learning theory we have critiqued in Chapter 2. We are championing the introduction of a literacies approach into future educational development partly as a means to bring subject and disciplinary issues back into consideration in areas where they have been in danger of being marginalized, but also because we believe there is a need for an alternative perspective to the technical-rational one which is currently driving institutional and governmental policy on higher education. In this we align our approach with that of other educational developers, such as Knapper:

> Educational developers have also played a vital role in keeping universities honest by drawing attention to the central *educational* mission of higher education at a time when our colleagues seem preoccupied with other matters – students with financing their education, faculty coping with increasing workloads and multiple demands on their time, and university presidents with public relations and fund-raising.
>
> (Knapper 2003: 7; emphasis added)

to which preoccupations we would add the demands of new e-learning technologies.

We see the educational development implications of this literacies-based challenge as having two necessary tracks. One is to bring the insights of language, text and discourse awareness to the attention of practitioners in the more conventionally cognitively-based traditions of learning technology development. The other is to bring to the attention of practitioners, interested in the development of writing in the mainstream university curriculum, issues around the relationship between academic literacies and new electronic communication practices. In so doing we continue to argue that written texts are at the heart of learning in higher education, whatever the technologies involved in curriculum delivery. Unfortunately, the possibilities for debates around e-learning and writing are limited by two dominant paradigms in educational development, which are having the effect of restricting further building on the kinds of pedagogic practice we have been exploring in this chapter. First, despite the evidence from both the research and practice we have drawn upon in this book, we still find that attention to student writing is frequently framed within a deficit model, rather than the academic literacies approaches explicated in Chapter 4. For example, a report published in the UK by the Royal Literary Fund 'communicates grave concerns about shortcomings in student writing skills' (Davies *et al.* 2006: vii). Extensive press coverage has been given to this report, fuelling suggestions of a fall in student standards of literacy and drawing upon the report itself to argue that this is directly linked to the fact that students inhabit a world of Internet downloading, text messaging and information overload, 'the new cultural forms that are moulding the consciousness of young people' (Davies *et al.* 2006: 11; see also the discussion of earlier public alarms about 'literacy crises' in Chapter 2). What was omitted in the press coverage was that the findings were primarily anecdotal, based on the experiences of a number of Royal Literary Fund 'writing fellows' who had been working with undergraduate students in different university settings. By its own admission, it was not an academic research report (Davies *et al.* 2006: vii), made scarcely any reference to the research in the international field of student writing or to UK-based academic literacies research and paid little attention to other educational developments in supporting student writing, apart from its own scheme.

The second dominant paradigm is that which we have referred to through-out the book, in which e-learning is decoupled from its subject-based and practice contexts and, consequently, also from the literacies and discourses which are implicitly embedded in its texts. Combining the 'student writing as deficit' discourse with the 'e-learning as technological competence' discourse, continues to legislate against engagement in the more complex textual understanding of learning in electronic environments which have been unpacked though the detail of the case studies explored in this chapter.

In order to address this, we suggest that educational developers should start by paying attention to the invisibility of writing (Lillis and Turner 2001) in the spaces where both these higher education arenas, writing and e-learning, intersect. One of these is the foregrounding of texts and their role in reflection, as evidenced in the case studies we have explored in this chapter. Research and practice in the field of reflective writing in higher education have their own history, raising questions about, for example, the tensions inherent in assessing personal forms of writing (Creme 2005) and the complex relationship between reflective writing and reflective practice in professional learning (Stierer 2000; Rai 2006). These debates are particularly relevant to current developments in teaching that address professional and practice-based contexts (such as the courses in our case studies) and to developments in e-learning which are responses to the turn towards professional development and lifelong learning, such as e-portfolio practices, as we will discuss in Chapter 6. Although concerned with more conventional contexts of teaching and learning in higher education, these debates are paying attention to issues which need to be drawn into our discussions around the textual dimension of e-learning practice, in particular because they foreground the relationship between the way in which knowledge is constructed and meanings are made through engagement in different kinds of texts. This offers a different interpretation of learning than that of assemblage, which tends to be the dominant focus in the e-portfolio movement (see Chapter 6). For example, Creme (2008) explores learning journals as 'transitional writing', a space for creativity and play as students reflect upon their understandings of disciplinary knowledge through their journal writing, which acts as a transitional space between their own experience and the formal texts of academic study and assessment, such as the objective and detached university essay. This kind of approach, with its focus on creativity, play and the association between different kinds of texts and understandings, can, we argue, be valuably applied to the assemblage of texts which are associated with e-learning portfolios, not merely as a technical process of uploading and ordering different text types but as integral to students' understanding and development of the construction of subject-based knowledge, or, as Creme suggests, a transitional space between the student's personal world and the more formal requirements of the curriculum, whether these be academic, professional or vocational.

We believe that e-learning can also benefit by drawing on other work which is exploring the connections between learning and student writing. An example of such an approach is provided by the 'Thinking Writing' programme at Queen Mary, London. This is a university-wide initiative, based upon the 'Writing in the Disciplines' programme developed at Cornell University (Monroe 2002), which is concerned with the ways in which writing constitutes particular 'ways of knowing, thinking, being and practicing within disciplinary and professional fields' (Mitchell 2006). Rather than seeing writing support as a separate add-on activity for students with problems, the programme is based on the premise that, in higher education, writing and learning are integral, and any attention to learning disciplines and subjects must involve attention to writing within the mainstream curriculum. The success of the approach is in part because of the central involvement of mainstream academic teachers who are embedding discipline and subject-specific writing work into the curriculum. Implicitly the project takes account of what literacies research has shown us, that written texts always embed particular social, cultural and institutional relationships of power and authority, and that in the university context these are often played out around what counts as subject-based and disciplinary knowledge, that is, issues of epistemology. Some of our own work following these principles has been briefly described earlier in this chapter in the section on the eWrite Site, and more detailed accounts have been given in Goodfellow and Lea (2005). Other activities related to the foregrounding of student writing in the university curriculum, and thus of relevance to the development of a literacies approach to e-learning, are proceeding through groups, such as the Interuniversity Academic Literacies Research Group at the Institute of Education   (http://ioewebserver.ioe.ac.uk/ioe/cms/get.asp?cid=5054&5054_0=6878 accessed March 2007) and the Writing Development in Higher Education conferences that have been held at a number of UK universities since 1994. An overview of these, and other writing development initiatives, can be found in Lea (2006).

6

The literacies of e-learning: research directions

Robin Goodfellow and Mary R. Lea

In our case studies, in the previous chapter, we described several contexts in which texts and technologies are constructed as sites for the development of students' creative and critical engagement with academic and professional practice. In all these cases the technologies, and the skills that the students needed to acquire in order to work with them, were subordinated to a focus on the texts, written and multimodal, that were the input to, and the outcome of, the work the students did. We showed how these texts encapsulated and represented whole systems of social action and relations between social actors, at the level of the classroom and the wider social worlds of the university and of professional practice. We highlighted the educational objective of the teachers and course developers, to bring these systems of action and relations into the conscious awareness of the students and make them subject to critical appraisal, and we described some of the pedagogical and technological means employed to make the texts that students consumed and produced accessible to this kind of critique. In considering the implications of this work for the kind of focus that educational developers would need to adopt in order to promote a text and literacies-based approach to e-learning across the curriculum more generally, we drew on the inspiration of work that has been going on in the field of student writing for a number of years. In particular, we referred to work on reflective writing which has explored the processes by which students' creative engagement with different kinds of writing helps them develop their understanding of the textual environment and the way that knowledge is constructed within it.

The case studies in Chapter 5 looked at student writing and other textual communication practices in the context of e-learning technologies that are common in university teaching in the anglophone world at present (multimedia portals, blogs, search engines, discussion boards). While we acknowledge that there is great variation in complexity and sophistication of systems and users to be found across the sector, we deliberately drew our examples from the kind of environments which represent a relatively modest level of development in technical infrastructure and know-how for the institutions themselves. This was in order to focus on the pedagogy rather than the technology as the principal locus of innovation. In reaction to the rhetoric that celebrates an e-learning-led 'revolution' in higher education, we have been concerned to bring the underlying and remarkably stable practices of the university as a generator of cultural capital into the picture, and to show how these continue to shape the textual productions of its teachers and students, however mediated the processes of production. In this final chapter we explore further some of the contradictions that challenge the successful integration of new media practices and established academic processes, with particular reference to an apparent contradiction that has risen within the discourses of e-learning itself, between the goal of efficient institutional management and accreditation of learning and the ideal of the fully independent and autonomous learner. We examine this dichotomy in the context of emerging practices, such as the giving away of learning materials free of charge ('open content'), and the use of electronic portfolio systems (e-portfolios) for assessment. We then discuss directions for the research that would inform the development of pedagogies that engage with students' textual practices across the range of communications media currently being promoted as resources for university learning and teaching.

E-learning for the management of learning or for learner empowerment?

In this book we have couched the challenge to e-learning largely in terms of resistance to learning technology as a dominant paradigm. In part this reflects interests generated from our own professional context. Our argument, advanced in Chapter 1, that the e-learning agenda focuses more on the management of learning than on the knowledge that it is supposed to construct, is part of an attempt to ameliorate the effects of a progressive sidelining of subject teaching and of academic discipline that we believe to be a consequence of an increasing institutional and governmental emphasis on technical innovation.

E-learning, however, is itself often promoted as a challenge to dominant higher education practice; this is evidenced by voices in the e-learning community who regret what they see as the continuing failure of new technologies to penetrate the established practice of some conventional universities and deliver the innovation in pedagogy and learning management which they believe it has promised for so long (Zemsky and Massey 2004; Hedberg 2006). Furthermore, as our discussion of technology as a site of educational practice has revealed, there is more than one 'paradigm' for e-learning, depending on whether it is being viewed from an institutional and management perspective, or through the visionary eyes of technology-inspired educational innovators. In our discussions so far, we have critiqued both the policy discourses which are driving the expanding allocation to universities of publicly funded resources for the development and implementation of tools and environments for the management of learning, and the innovation-driven arguments which claim to empower individual learners and their social networks to take control of their own learning, at the expense of all institutional control. What we turn our attention to now are emerging e-learning developments, such as the open courseware and e-portfolio movements (see below), which combine the apparently contradictory ideals of 'managing learning' and 'empowering learners' in an uncomfortable alliance ameliorated only by an expectation that new models for the university of the future will emerge somehow along with the emerging technologies.

Open courseware

The open courseware movement which has followed the initiative of the Massachusetts Institute of Technology (MIT) in making its course material freely available on the Internet (http://ocw.mit.edu), now involves over 100 higher education and other institutions around the world (http://www.ocwconsortium.org/about/index.shtml). There is evidence from MIT's evaluation of 2004 that a large number of organizations and individuals, including consortia of universities, have accessed and made use of the materials (MIT OpenCourseWare 2005), the largest number of visits appearing to be from individuals accessing MIT lecturers' notes. MIT does not offer any teaching or student support, and the initiative is presented on its website as a wholly philanthropic 'open dissemination of knowledge and information' (http://ocw.mit.edu/OcwWeb/Global/AboutOCW/our-story.htm accessed March 2007).

The Open University's own open courseware project, OpenLearn (http://www.open.ac.uk/openlearn/home.php), as in the case of MIT also part-funded by the Hewlett Foundation, similarly presents itself as a 'gift' to the world (http://www.open.ac.uk/openlearn/get-started-learner/case-studies.php#69 accessed March 2007), but in this case the focus is not on the materials as 'knowledge and information' but as 'designed to be studied flexibly by people who have a range of needs and experience' (http://www.open.ac.uk/openlearn/about-us/our-story.php accessed March 2007). The emphasis on learners, rather than on knowledge, is reinforced by the claim that it uses 'learning support and social networking tools to replicate the different informal modes of communication and learning that happen on a traditional campus' (http://www.open.ac.uk/openlearn/about-us/our-story.php).

As yet, there has been no suggestion that new teaching or learning practices are developing around either of these resources, and there is undoubtedly real educational value in the dissemination of high-prestige teaching material to people to whom it would previously have been inaccessible. Both initiatives are based on assumptions about learning, however, that are common to the e-learning paradigm of learner empowerment, but that we would wish to question from a literacies perspective. One, the MIT premise, is that knowledge resides in the teaching materials themselves, and that its dissemination around the world is a secondary matter of policy, finance and technology. The other, the OU position, is that learning resides in the replication of modes of communication that characterize traditional learning communities, and that these modes can be replicated by the use of electronic tools. These rhetorics position the donor universities as instruments of learner empowerment, but, from a literacies perspective, neither the materials nor the tools can be considered to be independent of the practices and values of the institutions that have produced them. Furthermore, for resources such as these to become sites in which learners can genuinely be empowered through engagement with the texts that they access, proper attention needs to be paid to the particular social and cultural contexts in which they will be read and used. To do this will require research, and both MIT and the OU have ongoing evaluation programmes for these projects (MIT OpenCourseWare 2005; McAndrew 2006). We are optimistic that these evaluations could include the kinds of investigation of context and communication that we have been conducting here (see Chapter 5). The scope and diversity of users of open courseware worldwide offers a remarkable opportunity for exploring both cultural and critical dimensions of academic literacies, as the texts produced as part of one set of institutional practices are appropriated and adapted to the needs of learners enculturated by another. However, we also acknowledge that it is possible, in the current economic climate of global higher education, that the open courseware movement will come to be seen by the provider institutions as the basis for a business model, in which the university simply embeds its teaching into models of the learner incorporated into the design of the materials through processes, such as Learning Design (see Chapter 2). Indeed, some have already suggested that this model will free up universities from teaching entirely, enabling them to focus only on the processes of accreditation, as learners draw their materials for study from open courseware sites (Greenberg 2006).

The open courseware movement therefore has ambivalent implications for a literacies approach to teaching and learning, as it is undoubtedly text-focused and oriented to independent learning, but is unlikely to be able to foster critical engagement with the material as long as the role of the teacher and the learning context is absent from its concerns. A similar ambivalence is also evident in the e-portfolio movement, even though it has a much more secure basis in pedagogy derived from a considerable pre-e-learning history of practice. The publicity materials of almost all the major commercial e-portfolio systems ally their development with moves towards the empowerment of learners, but at the same time much current e-portfolio practice is actually geared towards the institutional management of learning via processes of assessment and accreditation.

E-portfolios – practices and problems

E-portfolios are essentially repositories for digital material and content that users wish to collect and draw on in order to represent their educational and professional interests and achievements. While this kind of functionality has been available to universities ever since institutions first began to give their students personal websites, it is only relatively recently that the momentum for institutional e-portfolio systems has built up, following the successful marketing of commercial systems in the USA, the UK government's target of 'a personalised learning space, with the potential to support e-portfolios available within every college, by 2007–2008' (Department for Education and Skills 2005), and the establishment of consortia, such as the Electronic Portfolio Consortium (http://eportconsortium.org/), and the Open Source Portfolio project (http://www.osportfolio.org/). The momentum that has built up is considerable, along with an extensive literature, but it is noticeable that much of what is written about practice focuses on technological issues of most concern to institutions wishing to implement e-portfolios on an institution-wide basis, with all the issues of interoperability with existing systems that that implies. As Butler (2006: 1) observes in her extensive review of the literature, research in this field is fairly new, derives mainly from the learning and development of preservice teachers and does not tend to provide systematic accounts of practice (Challis 2005). One of the key practice-related issues that has been discussed extensively is reflection, because it is an arena of contrast between technicist and humanist approaches to personal development. Barrett and Carney (2005), for example, argue that the use of e-portfolios for summative assessment at institutional level, and for formative evaluation of learner reflection, are conflicting paradigms. Other researchers have raised issues with e-portfolios that resonate with the arguments we have been making in this book about the use of technologies to manage learning. For example, Tosh *et al.* (2005) report students' negative perceptions of e-portfolios because of a failure to relate the work involved to learning gains; Strivens (2005) discusses the increase in workload for both teachers and students involved in the presentation of portfolios for assessment; and Stefani (2005) draws attention to the limited use of these systems by teaching staff for their own professional development.

E-portfolios are therefore an important current locus of the intersection between academic literacy practices and e-learning technology. In this section, we will take a literacies lens to the kinds of practices they involve, and explore some of the contradictions that are implicit in their use for both students and teachers in university contexts. We will illustrate the discussion with examples from our own practice on the MA in Online and Distance Education programme.

The e-portfolio concept combines three familiar ideas. The first is the artist's portfolio, a receptacle in which representative samples of work are collected so that they can be carried around and shown to prospective exhibitors, buyers, employers, etc. This view of a portfolio seems unproblematic, but it does beg the question whether it is the work that determines the form of the receptacle (large prints require an equally large folder), or vice versa (you can only show work that fits into the folders available). In the case of a digital portfolio the receptacle is a computer, which, while it supports the collection and presentation of texts, images and audio files, also constrains the use of other types of artefact that might be produced in certain practice or research contexts: botanic samples, for example, or textile designs. The design of early e-portfolio systems based on student web pages, and that of some more recent systems developed as part of the Open Source movement, such as the OU's own Moodle-based system, aims to optimize user input, storage and retrieval of content without prejudging the kinds of presentation that might be made of it, if indeed it is to be presented at all. There is, however, an expectation that users will want to label and manage their material so that it can be easily exchanged between the e-portfolio system and the social media environments from which it is supposed that much of the content will come in future. This is done, for example, through the use of 'tags' to label content intuitively, rather than the more conventional file and folder structures that PC desktops use. Conceiving of e-portfolios as a way of recording informal social media activity resonates with the more radical and anti-institutional perspectives on e-learning that we have discussed above, but it is less compatible with the agendas of employability, quality assurance and professional accreditation regimes which view e-portfolio systems through the lens of benchmarking and assessment, as we discuss below. In either case, from a literacies perspective, the convergence of creative production and publishing activity around digital formats is neither a purely technical nor a socially neutral process, as the technologies themselves are inscribed with social meaning, power relations, possibilities for and restrictions on the expression of personal identity.

The second familiar practice underlying the notion of the e-portfolio is the personal diary or logbook, in which the writer plans, records and reflects on events in their everyday life in order to enhance their understanding and appreciation of their own experience. This use of portfolios, reflective logs and learning journals has of course been widespread in higher education for quite some time, including in many professional practice contexts, such as engineering, teaching and healthcare (see, for example, our discussion of the Wolverhampton PGCE in Chapter 5), in which learners are required to record and reflect on their experiences in order to develop professional skills and attitudes (Rai 2006). However, an apparently unproblematic practice again conceals ideological tensions. The privacy and individual ownership of a personal diary is clearly compromised if the contents of that diary are used by an institution as evidence for their author's competence to practice in a professional field, or otherwise to assess the quality and/or the process of their learning. Researchers and practitioners in reflective writing have been exploring and addressing these tensions around personal writing and its assessment in more conventional university curriculum contexts for some time (Stierer 2000; Bolton 2005; Creme 2005). Now the digitizing of portfolios makes the ownership issues even more complex, because digital contents are no longer in the physical possession of the author but are distributed across servers with privacy preserved only by a system of access permissions. The contemporary focus on performance outcomes has high-lighted the issue of who owns students' writing, and the development of e-portfolio systems able to extend and refine levels of access to it sharpens this further.

The third familiar practice behind the e-portfolio system is the school report, in which performance data and other information representing a learner's educational history are presented in a form that can be shared with parents, other schools, local authorities and employers at key stages of a learner's career. This idea is the one which has perhaps done most to drive e-portfolio developments at an institutional level, as it resonates most with the contemporary culture of performativity and accountability in education that we have touched on at various points in this book. In UK higher education the driver is the concept of the 'progress file' which is used to record educational achievement in a form that can be transferred between institutions and employers and across sectors, making a direct connection between evidence of a learner's performance and personal development, and information conveyed to institutions or employers for purposes of accreditation or employment (Quality Assurance Agency 2001b). The progress file and the professional development record may impose particular kinds of practice on the users of e-portfolio systems, such as the assessment of competences – specified areas of practice where a novice practitioner can be assessed as having met professional or occupational standards. However, literacy issues arise where textual indications of competence are decontextualized and reified into collections of digital 'evidence', losing in the process many of the markers that tie them to their original practice contexts (handwriting, for example, or other indications of transience in a textual artefact). When complex competences are deconstructed into lists of sub-skills and checked off against observable performance much of the 'evidence' that appears in the portfolio is in fact testimony that evidence has been provided (e.g. check-lists of key tasks done, countersigned by the practice mentor) rather than evidence of competency in its own right. In many practice contexts most of the relevant evidence is available only at the actual site of practice, demonstrated to the experienced practitioners whose responsibility it is to make the assessment of competence. However, in the translation from situated text to digital portfolio content, the record itself becomes the evidence. Mary has described a similar process working through the progress records completed by research students in Chapter 4.

Employers and organizations that have developed specifications for the skills and competences that they want their employees or trainees to acquire are pushing the use of e-portfolios to manage the recording and evidencing of these and other competences and qualifications acquired throughout a career. As a consequence there are many commercial and proprietorial software developers competing to build and sell e-portfolio systems which provide the functionality for standardized indices of performance to be evidenced, monitored, checked, assessed, stored and transmitted between stakeholders with an interest in accrediting learning. The requirement to generalize this kind of functionality spawns parallel activity in the software standards industry, with a proliferation of specifications and protocols competing to become the universal standard that all future systems will be required to adopt to ensure maximum interoperability across institutions and other contexts of use. The intensification of the marketing of technical 'solutions' to the student data management problem spins off into a competition among educational institutions not only to ensure that they are best placed to exploit any future standardization of e-portfolio accreditation processes, but also to present themselves to future customers as up-to-date and technologically visionary, in the now familiar pattern of the marketing of e-learning (see Chapter 1).

Thus e-portfolios are being used both to empower learners to 'take control' of their own learning, and also to assess their learning outcomes using standards and benchmarks required by external organizations. These apparently contradictory aims inflect the way that what are identified as the 'new skills' involved in collecting, recording and presenting digital information, and the more implicit underlying processes of reflection, planning, selection and evaluation, become part of the literacy practices of the courses and institutions which use them. Writing is implicated in this in a number of ways, as students are required to collect and store documents and other textual products generated in a variety of settings, including traditional academic writing done as part of coursework as well as content generated in more informal settings. While help with the technical processes of manipulating these texts in and out of different digital formats may be routinely provided by the institution or the software company which owns the e-portfolio system, support in negotiating the changing varieties of writing that the portfolio, as an expression of both practice and study contexts, requires from the student, is usually left to the teacher or mentor, who may themselves be struggling with the breadth of the textual genres evident in their students' e-portfolios.

The academic literacies of an e-portfolio course

Mary referred, in Chapter 4, to a basic question asked by some students on our own teaching programme, about how they should reference work collected in their e-portfolios and submitted for assessment. This is just one example of the issues that are being thrown up by the incorporation of fundamentally different assessment and evaluation practices from professional and occupational contexts into higher education. We have also experienced other related problems in our own practice around assessment, referencing, ownership of work, validation of authorship, admissibility of work produced elsewhere, quality of comment and reflection, level of academic engagement, appropriateness of genre, medium and register. All arose in the context of students' use of a variety of digital media and online communication practices to compile portfolios as evidence of their professional competency for a distance learning course at master's degree level, which is part of the Open University's MA in Online and Distance Education programme that we referred to in Chapter 5. We believe these problems to be indicative of the literacies issues that can be expected to confront university e-learning practitioners engaging with the coming age of social media and other manifestations of Web 2.0 (see Chapter 3). In particular, we want to highlight: the appropriating of digital content of different kinds to create the semblance rather than the substance of a piece of research; the presentation of records of participation in collaborative reflective activity as evidence of personal reflection; the adopting of popular media genres for academic purposes (e.g. the critical analysis of practice); and the integration of practice-based work from contexts external to the course. These issues all created problems of expectation and implementation both for the students, many of whom came to the course without any previous experience of either personal development planning, portfolios or collaborative online learning, and for the teachers, none of whom had assessed portfolio work before.

The course sets out to give practitioners, in higher and further education, the theoretical background and practical experience with technologies that would qualify them as professionals in the field of e-learning. As part of its approach, the course simulates a competences-based approach to the assessment of an e-portfolio of evidence. This simulation is solely for the purposes of discussion and debate, as there is no such competency framework for e-learning practitioners in the UK. A nominal framework for e-learning competences was created for the course, using the UK research councils' joint statement of research skills required by postgraduates as a model (UK Grad Programme 2001). The research councils' statement sets out 36 skills that research students are expected to be able to demonstrate, under seven general areas of competency: research skills and techniques; research environment; research management (which includes the use of information technology); personal effectiveness; communication skills; networking and teamworking; and, career management. The simulated 'e-learning competencies' framework for the course had just five competency areas: technology-related, communication-related, practice-related, research-related, and other-related. The students themselves were expected to propose specific skills which might be included in each of these categories. During the course, students were expected to compile an e-portfolio for assessment, consisting of items of 'evidence' of their achievement in each of the competency areas. This evidence was in the form of digital content: pieces of writing, websites, podcasts and other multimedia creations, entries to blogs, wikis and discussion forums, comments and references from tutors, colleagues and employers.

In addition to the examples of students' textual practices that we discuss below, the e-portfolio approach also produced a notable illustration of the power of conventional academic practice to shape learning processes so that they are perceived through the lens of established authority structures, regardless of the novelty of the technical environment. Although, as we have said, the 'e-learning competency' framework used for this course was not a real one, in that it did not represent an 'official' process of accreditation of e-learning practitioners, either by the university or by any external professional body, a number of students nevertheless took it as exactly that, and attempted to establish its precise requirements with regard to the more informal practices on the course, such as blogging and online discussion. These students experienced some frustration when their teachers would not provide more detail as to exactly how these competences were to be evidenced. Applying a literacies approach to this problem, and in anticipation of other difficulties arising for the teachers in marking the students' e-portfolios at several points throughout the course, the course developers produced a statement describing the kinds of text that could constitute evidence and the criteria for their assessment, which was made available to both students and teachers. This statement attempted to specify the amount and types of material (including comments on rhetorical features, such as audience and register) that could be included in the e-portfolio in the reasonable expectation of being carefully marked in the time available, and also the general areas in which quality would be judged. The following are examples of what they were required to demonstrate:

1. A range of activities through the e-portfolio. This required the use of a variety of forms of text (word documents, blogs, discussion forums, PowerPoint presentations, etc.). This criterion also attempted to specify the degree of modification of a piece of content that had already been assessed, for it to be submitted for a further assessment.
2. Engagement with course topics. This meant that the main themes of the course, such as reflection, theory and practice and multimedia, had to be explicitly addressed in some form, either through personal reflection or commentary.
3. Practical engagement with tools and technologies used on the course, either explicitly in the form of output created with the tools provided, or implicitly through demonstration of their understanding of practical issues that others face in their own use of technologies.
4. Intellectual engagement with ideas from the course. This was defined as evidence of original or critical thinking about ideas and theories encountered during the course, together with appropriate referencing.
5. Appropriate use and acknowledgement of collaboratively produced outcomes. Some of the evidence produced could contain elements of work that had been done collaboratively: a jointly-constructed wiki entry, an online dialogue, a blog page with responses, etc. Individual personal contribution to this work had to be made explicit.
6. Appropriate writing styles for all activities. This took in an understanding of audience and genre. The criteria distinguished primarily between

essays, reports, personal reflective writing and dialogic communication, such as messages to discussion forums. Clarity and coherence was required in all cases.

This statement and the assessment criteria attempted to reflect the practice orientation of the course, and the fact that those practices, despite the proliferation of technologies involved, are predominantly textual in nature. Working on a course about e-learning that uses e-learning, it was felt that the teachers needed to be supported in dealing with problems and misunderstanding arising from mismatches between the literacy practices of the course itself with its academic and disciplinary provenance, and those that students might bring in from their wider background in academia or professional education or from informal sites of use of the technologies that are employed. However, the number of problems that were generated by a cohort of just over 100 during the first 15-week presentation of the course was considerably more than anticipated, and the ongoing briefing of the tutors necessitated an online dialogue with the course developers that amounted to nearly 1000 messages. Here are some examples of the kinds of student activity and output that engaged the course teachers and developers in an almost continual discussion about the problems of assessment and how to deal with other tensions around the many different kinds of texts and practices that surfaced in the e-portfolios:

- Appropriation of digital content for semblance rather than substance. A group of students collaborates on the production of an interactive 'poster' using Adobe Acrobat, which represents the outcome of a research task on e-learning practice required by the course. The poster is attractively and competently designed using graphics, texts, figures, quotes, etc., reproduced from 35 sources internal and external to the course. These are all properly referenced, but the content is unstructured and simplistically presented through lists of illustrated bullet points elaborated only by broad headings and minimal comment. As a poster it works very well, as a summary of research it is woefully inadequate. Furthermore, it is clear that no permission has been sought for some of the corporate logos reproduced.
- Participation in collaborative reflection as evidence of personal reflection. Students submit e-portfolios for summative assessment which consist largely of extracts from dialogues with others on a range of course topics using a variety of technologies (wiki, podcast, discussion forum or blog). The dialogues show that the portfolio authors have been instrumental in facilitating discussion, but their personal contributions are not particularly insightful. Some also include overviews of their own thinking about reflection in multimodal formats, such as a coloured graphic of a mind-map containing branching themes and sub-themes, and labels in note form. These tend to describe rather than exemplify their authors' reflective thinking.
- Popular media genres used in academic tasks. Students create podcasts as part of a required task which asks them to critique an aspect of the

course that raises issues for e-learning in general. Most treat the assignment as a kind of audio-essay and approach it by writing themselves a
script which they then read into recorded format. Some use music to
introduce and play out. One or two conduct interviews with a second
party. In most cases the topics chosen are serious, addressing issues to do
with the educational use of technologies, such as blogging. One student,
however, treats the exercise as an opportunity to reflect on her personal
impressions of other students in her group. She adopts a homely and
humorous vocal delivery, which is highly entertaining and demonstrates
that she has observed and cleverly reproduced the style of a 'radio journal' broadcast. However, it has no explicit critical or otherwise analytic
content.

- Practice-based work integrated from external contexts. Some students
  submit e-portfolios for summative assessment, half of which consist of
  websites, presentations, research bids and course completion certificates
  which are the outcomes of previous career activities external to the
  course.

There are a large number of similar cases. It is not our intention to criticize
these students' outputs as such; in most cases the authors demonstrated
considerable technical skill and creative engagement. Nor have we space to
go into detail here about how these issues were addressed. The important
points are that these textual productions were generated by students getting
to grips with the technical (and competency-related) practices of the course,
but not with its implicit academic rationale or the expectations of its teachers
for written communication, deemed by them, with their own varied disciplinary backgrounds, as appropriate to study at master's degree level. The
tension between students' use of the e-portfolio as a vehicle for demonstrat-
ing that they had done what the course had asked them to do, and the course
developers' expectation that they would use it to construct a demonstration
of academic and professional achievement, had to be resolved *in situ* by
teachers who themselves felt insufficiently experienced in the different
pedagogical milieu of e-portfolio practice. This happened despite the e-
learning expertise and experience that went into the design, development
and teaching of the course, and the belated attempt by one of the course
team to bring a literacies perspective to the assessment of the e-portfolio.
The lessons learnt suggest that future development on this and similar
courses should give much more consideration to the nature of the digital
texts that the students will be producing, and their status and role as literacies within an institutionally academic environment. It may be that to do this
in a principled manner will require a level of understanding of the e-
portfolio as a site of pedagogical practice in the university that is only obtain-
able through a wider research programme.

Research directions

In presenting the case for a literacies perspective throughout this book we have drawn on research and practice across a range of different e-learning contexts, including web searching, online discussion, simulated case studies, blogs and e-portfolios. In a fast-changing world it is difficult to keep pace with new technological developments. Web 2.0 has been referred to throughout the book with the possibilities it offers for social networking, which are predicted to change the relationship of learners to their university studies. We need to be healthily wary of such claims because no doubt by the time of publication other applications will have appeared, and a year hence they may have been superseded by something else. It is important that in relation to ongoing research in this field we are suitably cautious about research – both in its method and findings – which is tied too closely to particular technological applications, unless it is able to unpack some general principles around texts, practices and e-learning. In this spirit we discuss here a possible agenda for researching in the broad field of digital literacies, raising questions that our arguments in this book have led us to ask and which we believe are missing from the general direction of e-learning research at the present time.

We have seen how during the last decade there has been a substantial investment in higher education in e-learning and, more recently, a rapid growth in the use of digital technologies and social networking among a generation who are regularly using these in their day-to-day lives. As a consequence, today's university students appear to be engaging with digital texts in ways that may seem far removed from the more conventional literacy demands of university study, but we actually know little about the ways in which literacies, learning and technologies intersect in students' lives as learners both within and outside the formal higher education curriculum. We believe that research in this area should be able to provide us with evidence of students' actual engagement with digital literacies, and respond to the lack of fine-grained ethnographic research of literacies, learning and technologies in higher education to date. It will also help to explore further the issues which Mary raised in Chapter 1, concerning the ways in which student learning is being reconfigured in university contexts through student participation in digital textual practice where spaces for disciplinary pedagogy and for the management of learning exist within one web-based interface. In addition, as new environments, such as Web 2.0, are able to offer possibilities for web 'readers' to become web 'writers' through forms of authorial textual practice, such as personal blogs and editable wikis, these too, are likely to have ongoing implications for universities in terms of who has the power to write and ownership over texts and concomitant implications for how we understand student learning. For example, a research project being carried out by Siân Bayne and Ray Land, 'Putting Web 2.0 to work: new pedagogies for new learning spaces', funded by the Higher Education Academy, is exploring how:

changed patterns of participation, responsibility and discernment ask the higher education community to engage with some far-reaching challenges relating to the literacies, pedagogies and assessment practices we bring to bear in these new digital spaces, and to the organisational contexts within which they are embedded.

(Personal email communication from S. Bayne, February 2007)

This is a new dimension for e-learning because it is concerned with a set of practices driven by students rather than designed by learning technologists. We suggest that, as a result, research in this area will need to adopt a rather different perspective than that which has been concerned with more traditional approaches to student learning, which have tended to focus on clear distinctions between outside/insider perspectives, concerning both what students do in university contexts and how to get students to adapt to academic practices and discourses (Hounsell 1988; Laurillard 1993). Now that the lived experience of being a student learner is cutting increasingly across a range of textual encounters and digital practices, we will need to turn our research attention to what happens when students bring their own textual interactions into the academy both through the use of text messaging, email and the Web on university computers and through social networking and file sharing sites, such as MySpace, Facebook, YouTube and Flickr. Indeed, instructional designers are increasingly attempting to draw on these online practices in the design of virtual learning spaces, as evidenced in the discussions around e-portfolios above. At the time of writing there has been little systematic research into students' textual encounters in social networking spaces and how they might be integrating these into more conventional curriculum literacy practices, for example, in the preparation of their assignments. We need to examine the ways in which students are engaging in digital textual practices as they move across all these different domains, blurring the boundaries of learning in and outside the formal curriculum. This posting from an undergraduate student to a BBC web page concerning the social networking site Facebook – which is particularly popular globally with university students – might suggest the shape of practices in the near future:

> Facebook has become a phenomenon at Nottingham University, so much so that I've decided to do my geography dissertation on it. Am in the process of just starting, and was worried that Facebook would just be a fad and my dissertation would be left high and dry, but it looks set to stay. Let's just hope I get to talk to the right people concerning it.
>
> Sally, Nottingham
> (BBC News Magazine, February, 2007: http://news.bbc.co.uk/1/hi/
> magazine/5109160.stm, accessed February 2007)

A recent research project, Learning from Digital Natives (in the early stages at the time of writing), has begun to examine students' digital activity in and outside the curriculum (http://www.academy.gcal.ac.uk/ldn/proj.html accessed February 2007). Looking primarily through a technological lens, it is exploring students' informal practices and examining their use of what are referred to as 'e-tools', such as mobile phones, digital cameras, iPods, computer games, Internet, blogs, and wireless technologies, in order to consider how these can be harnessed and brought into the academy. The method of inquiry for this project combines a literature review, focus groups with third-year undergraduate students in two subject areas in two different universities in Scotland, and interviews in the same institutions with teachers, managers and support staff. The projected project outcomes include a typology of barriers to and drivers of the integration of formal and informal learning using e-tools and case studies illustrating how to integrate formal and informal learning, using e-tools and policy guidelines and recommendations. The concern of this project is, then, specifically with providing an educational rationale for integrating formal and informal learning supported by e-tools and exploring how it might be possible to map this integration onto a new higher education curriculum. As a consequence the project is particularly concerned with the guidelines and recommendations that might be made to policy-makers, institutional managers, and teachers, about the ways in which e-tools can be used to support this kind of integration across different curriculum activities. As such, the project adopts an educational modelling approach, which appears to be based on the assumption that because students do certain kinds of things with technologies outside the curriculum, incorporating similar activities into the curriculum will somehow be able to enhance learning. However, as we saw in Chapter 2, there is no obvious one-to-one relationship between design for a technology and the way in which that technology is likely to be taken up in practice by students in particular contexts.

Research carried out by Conole *et al.* (2006) for the JISC (referred to in Chapter 3) explored students' experiences of e-learning, including what they do when they are learning with technologies and how they fit e-learning around their other more traditional learning activities. Although this project is not concerned specifically with the distinction between informal and informal learning, the findings do present evidence for the extensive use by students of a range of technologies and communicative tools, including mobile phones, laptop computers, personal digital assistants, USB memory sticks, email, MSN Chat and Skype. In addition, the project examined the use of standard computer software, such as Word, PowerPoint, Excel and statistical software, and use of the Web – discovering, perhaps not surprisingly, that, in most instances, this is students' first port of call for their studies. The findings conclude that there is a shift in the ways in which students are working as a direct result of the integration of tool use into their lives as learners. Data were collected across a range of subjects and disciplines in the first instance from a survey with 421 student respondents. In the second phase 85 students agreed to keep audio log diaries every time they used technologies to support learning activities. Fourteen of these students were interviewed in the final phase of data collection. Eight 'case study narratives' captured student experiences of using technologies in learning.

This is a very comprehensive study utilizing a variety of data collection methods and focusing primarily on student accounts of the use of technologies. Although methodologically it does take account of the socio-cultural setting, its still tends to concentrate upon perceived competence with tool use:

> Students are using technologies extensively to find, manage and produce content. They use technologies to support all aspects of their study. . .
>
> Students are sophisticated at finding and managing information (searching and structuring). They see the PC as their central learning tool. They are used to having easy access to information (for travel, entertainment, etc.) and therefore have an expectation of the same for their courses. . .
>
> There is a shift in the nature of the basic skills with a shift from lower to higher levels of [Bloom's] taxonomy, necessary to make sense of their complex technological enriched learning environment. . .
>
> Students are using tools in a combination of ways to suit individual needs. There is evidence of mixing and matching. They are comfortable with switching between media, sites, tools, content, etc. They said that technologies provide them with more flexibility in terms of being able to undertake learning anytime, anywhere.
>
> (Conole *et al.* 2006: 96)

Methodologically, neither of these projects appears to open up the possibility for exploring the more contested nature of learning that we suggest a literacies perspective, with its focus on texts as central to understanding meaning-making, would enable. There is generally little, if any, discussion of learning in terms of the different participants, or different interpretations of practices around technologies and the texts, which might be involved in any particular learning context. The one-to-one, transparent relationship between the tools and the learner is presented as self-evident, with the personal computer described as the central learning tool and other more mobile technologies providing the flexibility needed for students to undertake 'learning' anywhere, anytime. Concentrating on the tools, research findings are frequently represented through taxonomies of learning; an example of this can be found in Conole *et al.* (2007: 108). This seems to suggest that there is a transparent relationship between meaning-making and tool use.

However, it is not only this type of e-learning research that we are asking questions about. We also believe that there are limitations in much of the literacies research around technologies as it exists to date, primarily because of its tendency to valorize the multimodal and new media landscape (Kress 1998; Snyder 2001; Lankshear and Knobel 2003). As we saw in Chapter 4, this orientation to texts can result in a somewhat naïve view of the power of technology and the shift from page to screen to fundamentally change the literacies landscape and, we argue, tends to ignore the broader institutional context of textual production.

We suggest that in order to address the limitations of both e-learning research, in understanding textual practice, and the research which tends to foreground multimodality without taking due account of the specific landscape of tertiary education, we need to enlist other frameworks as heuristics, as ways of helping us to understand what is going on in e-learning contexts. This should help us to meet the challenge of researching the environments created when literacies and technologies intersect, or even collide. These frameworks share similar concerns for attention to the social and cultural dimensions of practice and can offer us complementary insights into the relation between literacies and technologies. For example, Russell (2002) outlines how activity theory can help us to recognize the mediating nature of language as a cultural tool. He argues that tools involve both different kinds of technologies and different mediated practices, which include language and other semiotic resources. We would include literacy practices, arguing that these could share a similar conceptual status to other mediated tools in an activity theory analysis. A further dimension is offered by work in the sociology of science and technology which underlies actor network theory (Latour and Woolgar 1979). This provides a framing which could bring literacies and technologies into the same 'heterogeneous networks' involving people, technologies, artefacts and texts working together. Particularly appealing in terms of researching e-learning, actor network theory does not distinguish between human actors and inanimate technologies in creating social contexts (Law 1992). In terms of the kinds of e-learning research we are proposing, there will always be an interrelationship between people, texts, practices and technologies, and it is this focus on interrelationship rather than on separate domains which we believe is an important dimension in any future research agenda. In addition, Lave and Wenger's (1991) concept of communities of practice has become ubiquitous in e-learning. We are particularly interested in how the ideas of 'reification' and 'participation', a dualism at the heart of Wenger's analysis in his later work (Wenger 1998), may be of particular value in researching literacies and technologies in higher education. He argues that all communities of practice produce reification in the form of abstractions, symbols, tools and concepts, and through this process practices take form. From this perspective we can see that both texts and technologies would present as different kinds of reifications, both being instantiations of institutional practice. We believe that, keeping our focus on texts but calling these perspectives more firmly into the research frame, we will be able to develop more nuanced ways of understanding the relationship between literacies, learning and technologies (Lea 2004b).

We have argued that, when associated with learning and assessment, technologies are always sites of textual practice and, therefore, we need to develop research methods which capture the textual as well as the technological. Our case studies in Chapter 5 presented an approach to practice, and it is imperative that we now go on to develop similar approaches in terms of research. As we have already argued, we believe that, such an approach is largely missing from the kinds of research projects discussed above and from the debates around e-learning research and method (Conole and Oliver 2007). Conole and Oliver have attempted to map out research in e-learning, exploring a range of approaches which bring together socio-cultural theories of learning; organizational structures; discussions around VLEs and learning objects; approaches to teaching with technologies; and e-assessment. The book is comprehensive and highlights some of the problems and difficulties facing the field, in particular its failure to develop a coherent discourse around learning. It also recognizes the problems of the 'toolbox' approach to theories and applications: 'The learning technology community has raided other disciplines' "toolboxes" without always recognizing the assumptions and values from which those tools have been developed' (Conole and Oliver 2007: 22). Contributors do take issue with much of the rhetoric around technologies (Oliver *et al.* 2007); nevertheless, there is still little engagement with why these technologies appear to be such drivers for change around learning. The focus tends to be on the 'e' rather than primarily upon learning. In addition, although research around power, control and surveillance is recognized, in terms of the mediating role of technologies in constructing identity and power relations, it is not given a central place on the agenda and so we are left wondering how this might be researched in more depth. One answer may be provided by Crook (2005), who argues that there is a need for more research at the intersection of academic literacies and new technologies, in particular with respect to reading texts within the broader contexts of institutional, technical and interpersonal practice which is, we argue, where power resides. We suggest that research which seeks to understand the complex relationships between these domains will need to take a primarily textual rather than technological lens to digital practices and consider how meanings are produced, negotiated and contested across modes and contexts, thus opening up for examination social relationships between the participants and the ways in which these are instantiated in the texts of e-learning. It would also take account of the deep historical and cultural association of the academy with the privileging of the written text and the fact that the institutional practice of being a student is still dominated by reading and writing texts, despite the fact that many of these are digital, hybrid and multimodal and open to manipulation in ways which have not been possible in the past. It would integrate some of the methods of inquiry and analysis which are being used to explore multimodality (often within school-based settings) and foreground the ways in which meanings are being realized through a range of modes, which are implicated in socially and culturally situated practices of reading and writing texts (Kress 2003b; Jewitt 2006). Axiomatic to any approach which draws together these complementary research perspectives is a recognition of the central nature of texts, both in the construction of knowledge and the practice of learning.

We need to find out more about the ways in which literacies, learning and technologies intersect in students' lives as learners, at the boundaries of, within and across, the formal curriculum. Research will need to explore the nature of digital literacies, the reading and writing practices which students are engaging with across and within different contexts. This kind of exploration of digital literacies should begin to tell us about the changing status of 'what counts' as knowledge around learning in today's higher education. This is particularly important since e-learning is blurring the distinctions between different kinds of academic and professional practice and between pedagogic practices and the institutional management and surveillance of learners – a change which is likely to have profound implications for how we come to view different types of knowledge in the future, possibly eliding the distinction between mode 1 and mode 2 knowledge production as presently defined.

The mix of modes, through which meanings are being realized, is already providing us with new challenges in analysing the relationship between texts which embed written, visual and aural elements. This raises both practical problems not only in terms of how best to store and analyse data but also how best to present and disseminate the outputs. As researchers, the boundaries which we have been used to working with around textual artefacts are changing; the conceptual categories we are familiar with are now more difficult to hold on to in this new research environment. For example, in academic literacies research, a case study might traditionally be framed by an individual research participant (a student) in a specific context (a university course), engaging in sets of discrete texts (student essays/tutor feedback). Working with digital texts and practices in e-learning contexts, the boundaries between these are more blurred and continually being redefined – a process which is likely to accelerate in the future. For example, an analysis of how students negotiate meanings over an assignment may include data from text messages, from student postings on a social networking site, such as Facebook Notes, and MSN chat; in addition, the student may enter into an email dialogue with his or her tutor about the assignment, requesting advice on using an attached visual and the tutor offering a web link to a relevant site. The challenge for us, as researcher practitioners, is going to be how to present meaningful research outputs with this type of data within a dominant model which foregrounds the academic published text, such as books and journal articles. We are going to have to find ways of organizing our data in relation to particular forms of research output, including journal articles, web resources, interactive visual presentations, electronic publications, podcasts and research blogs. Future research in literacies and technologies will require us to bring together different conceptual frames for collection, analysis and dissemination in the research process.

Summary and conclusion

In this book we have asked whether technological agendas, policies and practices will inevitably be decoupled from, and seen in tension with, more traditional disciplinary concerns around established authoritative knowledge bases. The tendency in the e-learning field to focus on constructivism and knowledge construction, gaming, mobile technologies, learning objects and multimedia applications, seems to suggest that this is the case. E-learning is also often closely aligned with concomitant shifts towards professional and vocational fields of study, coupled with the reflective turn in assessment. We are curious as to why this is and wonder if courses in these areas perhaps offer less of a challenge than the integration of e-learning into more conventional subjects, apart, that is, from the use of repositories for accessing online resources, lecture notes, etc. We suggest that e-learning research agendas need to embrace the broader contexts of higher education's disciplinary fields, and that a literacies framing is particularly well placed to do so because of its theoretical and methodological orientation which pay particular attention to the construction of disciplinary knowledge across and within different contexts.

Using a social literacies perspective to examine the policies and practices of e-learning in the university, has exposed issues that we believe need to be addressed if we are to reconcile the traditional disciplinary focus of teaching and learning in higher education with the twenty-first century demands of the professional curriculum, lifelong learning and new media practices. Looking through this lens at the e-learning policy statements, of UK national higher education agencies, leads us to view them as discourses that work together to reconfigure the university's role in the global knowledge economy, constituting it primarily as one of managing the support and development of learner/customers in the interests of their current or future employers, rather than as facilitating their independent access to bodies and systems of knowledge. These discourses, we argue, sit in an uneasy relation to universities' traditional view of themselves as centres of disciplinary expertise, and to views of student learning that focus on the epistemological dimensions of engagement with bodies of knowledge.

References

Alexander, B. (2006) Web 2.0: a new wave of innovation for teaching and learning? *EDUCAUSE Review*, 41(2). http://www.educause.edu/apps/er/erm06/erm0621.asp (accessed March 2007).

Anderson, C. (2005) Mainstream media meltdown, *The Long Tail*. http://longtail.typepad.com/the_long_tail/2005/04/media_meltdown.html (accessed March 2007).

Anderson, J.R. (1996) ACT: a simple theory of complex cognition, *American Psychologist*, 51, 355–65.

Ashley, J. (2006) New technology may be changing the human brain, *The Guardian*, 24 April. http://www.guardian.co.uk/comment/story/0,,1759704,00.html#article_continue (accessed January 2007).

Ashwin, P. and McLean, M. (2004) Towards a reconciliation of phenomenographic and critical pedagogy perspectives in higher education through a focus on academic engagement, in C. Rust (ed.) *Improving Student Learning: Diversity and Inclusivity*. Oxford: Oxford Centre for Staff Development, pp. 377–89.

Ausubel, D. (1968) *Educational Psychology: A Cognitive View*. New York, NY: Holt, Rinehart and Winston.

Ballard, B. and Clanchy, J. (1988) Literacy in the university: an 'anthropological' approach, in G. Taylor, B. Ballard, V. Beasley, H.K. Bock, J. Clanchy and P. Nightingale (eds) *Literacy by Degrees*. Milton Keynes: Society for Research into Higher Education/Open University Press, pp. 7–23.

Barab, S.A. and Duffy, T.M. (2000) From practice fields to communities of practice, in D. Jonassen and S. Land (eds) *Theoretical Foundations of Learning Environments*. Mahwah, NJ: Lawrence Erlbaum Associates, pp. 25–55.

Barab, S., Makinster, J., Moore, J. and Cunningham, D. (2001) Designing and building an online community: the struggle to support sociability in the Inquiry Learning Forum, *Educational Technology Research and Development*, 49(4), 71–96.

Barnett, R. (1997) *Higher Education: A Critical Business*. Buckingham: Society for Research into Higher Education/OpenUniversity Press.

Barrett, H. (2004) Electronic portfolios as digital stories of deep learning: emerging digital tools to support reflection in learner-centred portfolios. http://electronicportfolios.com/digistory/epstory.html (accessed March 2007).

Barrett, H. and Carney, J. (2005) Conflicting paradigms and competing purposes in electronic portfolio development. http://electronicportfolios.com/portfolios/LEAJournal-BarrettCarney.pdf (accessed March 2007).

Bartholomae, D. (1986) Inventing the university, in M. Rose (ed.) *When a Writer Can't Write: Studies in Writer's Block and Other Composing-Process Problems.* New York, NY: Guilford Press, pp. 134–66.

Barton, D. (1994) *Literacy: An Introduction to the Ecology of Written Language.* Oxford: Blackwell.

Barton, D. and Hamilton, M. (1998) *Local Literacies: Reading and Writing in One Community.* London: Routledge.

Barton, D., Hamilton, M. and Ivanič, R. (eds) (1994) *Worlds of Literacies.* Clevedon: Multilingual Matters.

Bayne, S. (2006) Networked learning with digital texts. Paper presented to Networked Learning Conference, University of Lancaster, 10–12th April. http://www.networkedlearningconference.org.uk/abstracts/pdfs/P13%20Bayne.pdf (accessed March 2007).

Baynham, M. and Prinsloo, M. (2001) New directions in literacy research, *Language and Education*, 15(2–3), 83–91.

Bazerman, C. (1988) *Shaping Written Knowledge: The Genre and Activity of the Experimental Article in Science.* Madison: University of Wisconsin Press.

Beaudoin, M. (2002) Learning or lurking? Tracking the 'invisible' online student, *The Internet and Higher Education*, 5, 147–55.

Berge, Z. and Collins, M. (1995) Computer-mediated communication and the online classroom: overview and perspectives, *Computer-Mediated Communication Magazine.* http://www.december.com/cmc/mag/1995/feb/berge.html (accessed March 2007).

Berkenkotter, C. and Huckin, T. (1995) *Genre Knowledge in Disciplinary Communication.* Hillsdale, NJ: Lawrence Erlbaum Associates.

Bizzell, P. (1982) Cognition, convention and certainty: what we need to know about writing, *PRE TEXT*, 3(3), 213–44.

Blommaert, J. (2005) *Discourse: A Critical Introduction.* Cambridge: Cambridge University Press.

Bloom, B., Englehart, M., Furst, E., Hill, W. and Krathwohl, D. (1956). *Taxonomy of Educational Objectives: The Classification of Educational Goals. Handbook I: Cognitive Domain.* New York, NY: Longmans, Green.

Bolter, D.J. and Grusin, R. (1999) *Remediation: Understanding New Media.* Cambridge, MA: MIT Press.

Bolton, G. (2005) *Reflective Practice: Writing and Professional Development*, 2nd edn. London: Sage.

Bonk, C. and King, K. (1998a) Introduction, in C. Bonk and K. King (eds) *Electronic Collaborators: Learner-Centered Technologies for Literacy, Apprenticeship and Discourse.* Mahwah, NJ: Lawrence Erlbaum Associates, pp. xxv–xxxv.

Bonk, C. and King, K. (eds) (1998b) *Electronic Collaborators: Learner-Centered Technologies for Literacy, Apprenticeship and Discourse.* Mahwah, NJ: Lawrence Erlbaum Associates.

Bourdieu, P. (1977) *Outline of a Theory of Practice.* Cambridge: Cambridge University Press.

British Educational Communications and Technology Agency (2001) The 'digital divide': a discussion paper. http://www.becta.org.uk/page_documents/research/digitaldivide.pdf (accessed May 2007).

Britton, J. (1970) *Language and Learning.* Miami, FL: University of Miami Press.

Brookfield, S.D. (1995) *Becoming a Critically Reflective Teacher.* San Francisco, CA: Jossey-Bass.

Brown, J.S. and Duguid, P. (2000) *The Social Life of Information.* Boston, MA: Harvard Business School Press.

Brown, J.S., Collins, A. and Duguid, P. (1989) Situated cognition and the culture of learning, *Educational Researcher,* 18, 32–42.

Bruner, J., Goodnow, J. and Austin, A. (1956) *A Study of Thinking.* New York, NY: Wiley.

Burbules, N.C. (2000) Does the Internet constitute a global educational community? in N.C. Burbules and C. Torres (eds) *Globalisation and Education: critical perspectives.* London: Routledge. pp. 323–56.

Butler, P. (2006) A review of the literature on portfolios and electronic portfolios. http://www.elearnspace.org/blog/archives/002718.html (accessed May 2007).

Carmichael, P., Goodfellow, R. and Thorpe, M. (2005) Contexts, communities and networks: mobilizing learners' resources and relationships in different domains. ESRC Teaching and Learning Research Programme Thematic Seminar Series, Seminar Three. http://crll.gcal.ac.uk/docs/TLRP_ContextSeminars/TLRP_ContxtSem3_Thorpeetal.doc (accessed February 2007).

Castells, M. (1996) *The Rise of the Network Society.* Oxford: Blackwell.

Challis, D. (2005) Towards the mature ePortfolio: some implications for higher education, *Canadian Journal of Learning and Technology,* 31(3). http://www.cjlt.ca/content/vol31.33/challis.html (accessed March 2007).

Coffin, C. and Hewings, A. (2005) Language learning and electronic communications media, *International Journal of Educational Research,* 43(7–8), 427–31.

Collis, B. (1996) *Tele-learning in a Digital World: The Future of Distance Learning.* London: International Thompson Computer Press.

Conole, G., de Laat, M., Dillon, T. and Darby, J. (2006) JISC LXP: Student experiences of technologies: Final report. http://www.jisc.ac.uk/media/documents/programmes/elearning_pedagogy/lxp%20project%20final%20report%20dec%202006.pdf (accessed January 2007).

Conole, G. and Oliver, M. (eds) (2007) *Contemporary Perspectives in E-learning Research: Themes, Methods and Impact on Practice.* London: Routledge.

Conole, G., Oliver, M., Falconer, I., Littlejohn, A. and Harvey, J. (2007) Designing for learning, in G. Conole and M. Oliver (eds) *Contemporary Perspectives in E-learning Research: Themes, Methods and Impact on Practice.* London: Routledge, pp. 101–20.

Cook-Gumperz, J. (ed.) (1986) *The Social Construction of Literacy.* Cambridge: Cambridge University Press.

Cope, B. and Kalantzis, M. (eds) (1999) *Multiliteracies: Literacy Learning and the Design of Social Futures.* London and New York: Routledge.

Cornford, J. and Pollock, N. (2002) The university campus as a 'resourceful constraint': process and practice in the construction of the virtual university, in M.R. Lea and K. Nicoll (eds) *Distributed Learning: Social and Cultural Approaches to Practice.* London and New York: RoutledgeFalmer, pp. 170–81.

Creme, P. (2000) The 'personal' in university writing: uses of reflective learning journals, in M.R. Lea and B. Stierer (eds) *Student Writing in Higher Education: New Contexts.* Buckingham: Society for Research into Higher Education/Open University Press, pp. 97–111.

Creme, P. (2005) Should student learning journals be assessed? *Assessment and Evaluation in Higher Education,* 30(3), 287–96.

Creme, P. (2008) Transitional writing: a space for academic play, *Arts and Humanities in Higher Education,* 7(1).

Crook, C. (1994) *Computers and the Collaborative Experience of Learning.* London and New York: Routledge.

Crook, C. (2002) Learning as cultural practice, in M. Lea and K. Nicoll (eds) *Distributed Learning: Social and Cultural Approaches to Practice.* London and New York: RoutledgeFalmer, pp. 152–69.

Crook, C. (2005) Addressing research at the intersection of academic literacies and new technology, *International Journal of Educational Research,* 43(7–8), 509–18.

Crowley, S. (1995) Composition's ethic of service, the universal requirement and the discourse of student need, *JAC (Journal of Advanced Composition),* 15(2): 227–39.

Davidson, G. and Lea, M. (1994) *Modularity.* Technical Issues Paper, Further Education Unit.

Davies, S., Swinburne, D. and Williams, G. (eds) (2006) *Writing Matters: The Royal Literary Fund Report on Student Writing in Higher Education.* London: Royal Literary Fund.

Deacon, H., Walton, M. and Wilson, F. (1997) Developing multimedia for higher education – the experience of the Isiseko Project. Paper presented at the Future World Conference, University of Capetown, 3 December.

Delanty, G. (2001) *Challenging Knowledge: The University in the Knowledge Society.* Buckingham: Society for Research into Higher Education/Open University Press.

Department for Education and Employment (1998) *The Learning Age: A Renaissance for a New Britain.* London: The Stationery Office. http://www.lifelonglearning. co.uk/greenpaper/ (accessed May 2007).

Department for Education and Skills (2005) Raising standards: a contextual guide to support success in literacy, numeracy and ESOL provision. http:// www.dfes.gov.uk/readwriteplus/raisingstandards/elearning/introduction/ (accessed March 2007).

Dewey, J. (1938) *Experience and Education.* New York, NY: Macmillan.

Dewey, J. (1998) *How We Think.* Houghton: Mifflin Company. Revised edition first published in 1933.

Doherty, C. (2004) Promising virtues in the virtual classroom: metaphors on trial, in E. McWilliam, S. Danby and J. Knight (eds) *Performing Research: Theories, Methods and Practices,* Flaxton, Qld.: Post Pressed.

Downes, S. (2001) Learning objects: resources for distance education worldwide, *International Review of Research in Open and Distance Learning,* 2(1). http://www. irrodl.org/index.php/irrodl/article/view/32/81 (accessed May 2007).

Downes, S. (2006) E-learning 2.0, *eLearn Magazine.* http://www.elearnmag.org/ subpage.cfm?section=articles&article=29–1 (accessed March 2007).

Durrent, C. and Green, B. (1998) *Literacy and the New Technologies in School Education: Meeting the L(IT)eracy Challenge?* NSW Department of Education and Training, Sydney.

Engeström, Y. (1990) *Learning, Working and Imagining: Twelve Studies in Activity Theory.* Helsinki: Orienta-Konsultit.

Fairclough, N. (1992) *Discourse and Social Change.* Cambridge: Polity Press.

Fairclough, N. (2000) *New Labour, New Language?* London: Routledge.

Fairclough, N. (2001) *Language and Power,* 2nd edn. London and New York: Longman.

Fisher, D. (2006) Remediating the professional classroom: The new rhetoric of teaching and learning. Unpublished PhD thesis, Iowa State University, USA. http:// mycase.engl.iastate.edu/presentations/present.cfm (accessed December 2006).

Flower, L. and Hayes, J. (1981) A cognitive theory of writing, *College Composition and Communication*, 32, 365–87.

Garrick, J. and Jakupec, V. (eds) (2000) *Flexible Learning, Human Resource and Organisational Development: Putting Theory to Work.* London: Routledge.

Garrison, R., Anderson, T. and Archer, W. (2001) Critical thinking, cognitive presence and computer conferencing in distance education, *American Journal of Distance Education*, 15(1), 7–23.

Gee, J.P. (1992) *The Social Mind: Language, Ideology and Social Practice.* New York, NY: Bergin and Garvey.

Gee, J.P. (1996) *Social Lingustics and Literacies: Ideology in Discourse.* London: Falmer Press.

Gee, J.P. (2000) The new literacy studies: from 'socially situated' to the work of the social, in D. Barton, M. Hamilton and R. Ivanič (eds) *Situated Literacies: Reading and Writing in Context.* London and New York: Routledge, pp. 180–96.

Gee, J.P. (2005) *An Introduction to Discourse Analysis: Theory and Method*, 2nd edn. London and New York: Routledge.

Gibbons, M., Limoge, C., Nowotny, H., Schwartzman, S., Scott, P. and Trow, M. (1994) *The New Production of Knowledge: The Dynamic of Science and Research in Contemporary Societies.* London: Sage.

Gibbs, G. (ed.) (1994) *Improving Student Learning: Theory and Practice.* Oxford: Oxford Centre for Staff Development.

Gibbs, G. (1995) *Learning in Teams: Tutor Guide.* Oxford: Oxford Centre for Staff Development.

Goldhaber, M. (1997) The attention economy and the Net. *FirstMonday*, 2(4). http://www.firstmonday.org/issues/issue2_4/goldhaber/index.html (accessed January 2007).

Goodfellow, R. (2001) Credit where it is due: assessing students' contributions to collaborative online learning, in D. Murphy, R. Walker and G. Webb (eds) *Online Learning and Teaching with Technology.* London: Kogan Page, pp. 73–80.

Goodfellow, R. (2004a) The literacies of online learning: a linguistic-ethnographic approach to research on virtual communities, in S. Banks, P. Goodyear, V. Hodgson, C. Jones, V. Lally, D. McConnell and C. Steeples (eds) *4th Networked Learning Conference.* University of Lancaster, April. http://www.networkedlearningconference.org.uk/past/nlc2004/proceedings/symposia/symposium7/goodfellow.htm (accessed May 2007).

Goodfellow, R. (2004b) Online literacies and learning: operational, cultural and critical dimensions, *Language and Education*, 18(5), 379–99.

Goodfellow, R. (2005a) Virtuality and the shaping of educational communities, *Education, Communication & Information*, 5(2), 113–29.

Goodfellow, R. (2005b) Academic literacies and e-learning: a critical approach to writing in the online university, *International Journal of Educational Research*, 43(7–8), 481–94.

Goodfellow, R. (2006) From 'equal access' to 'widening participation': the discourse of equity in the age of e-learning, in J. Lockard and M. Pegrum (eds) *Brave New Classrooms, Eduational Democracy and the Internet.* New York, NY: Peter Lang, pp. 55–74.

Goodfellow, R. and Hewling, A. (2005) Reconceptualizing culture in virtual learning environments: from an 'essentialist' to a 'negotiated' perspective, *E-learning*, 2(4), 356–68.

Goodfellow, R. and Lea, M.R. (2005) Supporting writing for assessment in online learning, *Assessment and Evaluation in Higher Education*, 30(3), 261–71.

Goodfellow, R., Lea, M., Gonzalez, F. and Mason, R. (2001) Opportunity and e-quality: intercultural and linguistic issues in global online learning, *Distance Education*, 22(1), 65–84.

Goodfellow, R., Morgan, M., Lea, M. and Pettit, J. (2004) Students' writing in the virtual university: an investigation into the relation between online discussion and writing for assessment, in I. Snyder and C. Beavis (eds) *Doing Literacy Online: Teaching, Learning and Playing in an Electronic World*. Creskill, NJ: Hampton Press, pp. 25–44.

Greenberg, J. (2006) Unlocking access to learning at the Open University with OpenLearn: an interview with Joel Greenberg of the UK's OU, *IMS Series on Learning Impact*. http://www.imsproject.org/articles/getpdf.cfm?DocName=15Dec2006Greenberg.pdf (accessed March 2007).

Haggis, T. (2003) Constructing images of ourselves? A critical investigation into 'approaches to learning' research in higher education, *British Educational Research Journal*, 29(1), 89–104.

Halliday, M.A.K. (1978) *Language as Social Semiotic*. London: Edward Arnold.

Hansell, S. (2006) For MySpace, making friends was easy. Big profit is tougher, *New York Times*, 23 April. http://www.nytimes.com/2006/04/23/business/yourmoney/23myspace.html?ei=5090&en=68344369c2b006ac&ex=1303444800&partner=rssuserland&emc=rss&pagewanted=all (accessed March 2007).

Harasim, L. (1989) Online education: a new domain, in R. Mason and T. Kaye (eds) *Mindweave: Communication, Computers and Distance Education*. Oxford: Pergamon, pp. 50–62.

Haythornthwaite, C. (2002) Building social networks via computer networks: creating and sustaining distributed learning communities, in K. Renninger and W. Shumar (eds) *Building Virtual Communities: Learning and Change in Cyberspace*. Cambridge: Cambridge University Press, pp. 159–90.

Heath, S.B. (1983) *Ways with Words: Language, Life and Work in Communities and Classrooms*. Cambridge: Cambridge University Press.

Hedberg, J. (2006) E-learning futures? Speculations for a time yet to come, *Studies in Continuing Education*, 28(2), 171–83.

Herring, S. (2001) Computer-mediated discourse, in D. Tannen, D. Schiffrin and H. Hamilton (eds) *The Handbook of Discourse Analysis*. Oxford: Blackwell, pp. 612–34.

Higher Education Funding Council for England, Joint Information Systems Committee and Higher Education Academy (2005) HEFCE strategy for e-learning. http://www.hefce.ac.uk/pubs/hefce/2005/05_12/ (accessed May 2007).

Hoare, S. (2002) Not good at sums, *The Guardian*, 26 November. http://education.guardian.co.uk/specialreports/tuitionfees/story/0,,847501,00.html (accessed January 2007).

Hounsell, D. (1988) Towards an anatomy of academic discourse: meaning and context in the undergraduate essay, in R. Säljö (ed.) *The Written World: Studies in Literate Thought and Action*. Berlin: Springer-Verlag, pp. 161–77.

Hughes, J. and Edwards, J. (2005) Becoming an ePortfolio learner and teacher. Paper presented to EiFel International ePortfolio Conference, University of Cambridge, October.

Ivanič, R. (1998) *Writing and Identity: The Discoursal Construction of Identity in Academic Writing*. Amsterdam: John Benjamins.

Ivanič, R., Clark, R. and Rimmershaw, R. (2000) What am I supposed to make of this? The messages conveyed to students by tutors' written comments, in M.R. Lea and B. Stierer (eds) *Student Writing in Higher Education: New Contexts*. Buckingham: Society for Research into Higher Education/ Open University Press, pp. 47–65.

Jenkins, R. (1992) *Pierre Bourdieu*. London and New York: Routledge.

Jewitt, C. (2006) *Technology, Literacy and Learning: A Multimodal Approach*. London: Routledge.

Jonassen, D.H. and Land, S.M. (eds) (2000) *Theoretical Foundations of Learning Environments*. Mahwah, NJ: Lawrence Erlbaum Associates.

Jonassen, D.H., Mayes, T. and MacAleese, R. (1993) A manifesto for constructivist approaches to the use of technology in higher education, in T.M. Duffy, J. Lowyck and D.H. Jonassen (eds) *Design Environments for Constructive Learning*. New York, NY: Springer-Verlag, pp. 231–47.

Jones, C., Turner, J. and Street, B. (eds) (1999) *Students Writing in the University: Cultural and Epistemological Issues*. Amsterdam: John Benjamins.

King, K. (1998) Designing 21st-century educational networlds: structuring electronic social spaces, in C. Bonk and K. King (eds) *Electronic Collaborators: Learner-Centered Technologies for Literacy, Apprenticeship and Discourse*. Mahwah, NJ: Lawrence Erlbaum Associates, pp. 365–84.

Knapper, C. (2003) Three decades of educational development, *International Journal for Academic Development*, 8(1–2), 5–9.

Koper, R. (2005) Modelling lifelong learning networks. Presentation to IPSI Conference, 30 April. http://dspace.ou.nl/handle/1820/331 (accessed February 2007).

Krause, K.-L. (2006) Who is the E generation and how are they fairing in higher education? in J. Lockard and M. Pegrum (eds) *Brave New Classrooms: Democratic Education and the Internet*. New York, NY: Peter Lang, pp. 125–40.

Kress, G. (1998) Visual and verbal modes of representation in electronically mediated communication: the potentials of new forms of text, in I. Snyder (ed.) *Page to Screen: Taking Literacy into the Electronic Era*. St Leonards, NSW: Allen & Unwin, pp. 53–79.

Kress, G. (2001) Writing, knowing and learning in the era of multimodality. Keynote paper presented to the International Literacy Conference, Literacy and Language in Global and Local Settings: New Directions for Research and Teaching, University of Cape Town, 13–17 November.

Kress, G. (2003a) Design and transformation: new theories of meaning, in B. Cope and M. Kalantzis (eds) *Multiliteracies: Literacy Learning and the Design of Social Futures*. London and New York: Routledge.

Kress, G. (2003b) *Literacy in the New Media Age*. London: Routledge.

Kress, G. and van Leeuwen, T. (2001) *Multimodal Discourse: The Modes and Media of Contemporary Communication*. London: Arnold.

Kress, G. and Street, B. (2006) Foreword, in K. Pahl and J. Rowsell (eds) *Travel Notes from the New Literacy Studies*. Clevedon: Multilingual Matters, pp. vii–x.

Language and Education (2001) New directions in literacy research: policy, pedagogy and practice, *Language and Education*, 15(2–3).

Lankshear, C. and Knobel, M. (2003) *New Literacies: Changing Knowledge and Classroom Learning*. Maidenhead: Open University Press.

Lankshear, C. and Knobel, M. (2004) Text-related roles of the digitally 'at home'. Paper presented to the American Educational Research Association, San Diego,

15 April. http://www.geocities.com/c.lankshear/roles.html (accessed March 2007).

Lankshear, C., Peters, M. and Knobel, M. (2002) Information, knowledge and learning: some issues facing epistemology and education in a digital age, in M.R. Lea and K. Nicoll (eds) *Distributed Learning: Social and Cultural Approaches to Practice.* London and New York: RoutledgeFalmer, pp. 16–37.

Lankshear, C., Snyder, I. and Green, B. (2000) *Teachers and Techno-literacy: Managing Literacy, Technology and Learning in Schools.* St Leonards, NSW: Allen & Unwin.

Latour, B. and Woolgar, S. (1979) *Laboratory Life: The Social Construction of Scientific Facts.* Beverley Hills, CA: Sage.

Laurillard, D. (1993) *Rethinking University Teaching.* London and New York: Routledge.

Lave, J. and Wenger, E. (1991) *Situated Learning: Legitimate Peripheral Participation.* Cambridge: Cambridge University Press.

Law, J. (1992) Notes on the theory of actor network. Science Studies Centre, University of Lancaster.

Lea, M.R. (1994) 'I thought I could write until I came here': Student writing in higher education, in G. Gibbs (ed.) *Improving Student Learning: Theory and Practice.* Oxford: Oxford Centre for Staff Development, pp. 216–26.

Lea, M.R. (1998) Academic literacies and learning in higher education: constructing knowledge through texts and experience, *Studies in the Education of Adults,* 30(2), 156–71.

Lea, M.R. (2000) Computer conferencing: new possibilities for writing and learning in higher education, in M.R. Lea and B. Stierer (eds) *Student Writing in Higher Education: New Contexts.* Buckingham: Society for Research into Higher Education/Open University Press, pp. 69–85.

Lea, M.R. (2001) Computer conferencing and assessment: new ways of writing in higher education, *Studies in Higher Education,* 26(2), 163–182.

Lea, M.R. (2004a) Academic literacies: a pedagogy for course design, *Studies in Higher Education,* 20(6), 738–56.

Lea, M.R. (2004b) The New Literacy Studies, ICTs, and Learning, in L. Snyder and C. Beavis (eds) *Doing Literacy Online: Teaching, Learning and Playing in an Electronic World.* Cresskill, NJ: Hampton Press.

Lea, M.R. (2005) Communities of practice in higher education: useful heuristic or educational model? in D. Barton and K. Tusting (eds) *Beyond Communities of Practice: Language, Power and Social Context.* Cambridge: Cambridge University Press, pp. 180–97.

Lea, M.R. (2006) Writing in today's university, *Magazine of the Staff and Educational Development Association (SEDA),* November: 1–3.

Lea, M.R. (forthcoming) Emerging literacies in online learning, *Journal of Applied Linguistics.*

Lea, M.R. and Stierer, B. (eds) (2000) *Student Writing in Higher Education: New Contexts.* Buckingham: Society for Research into Higher Education/Open University Press.

Lea, M.R. and Street, B.V. (1998) Student writing in higher education: an academic literacies approach, *Studies in Higher Education,* 23(2), 57–72.

Lea, M.R. and Street, B.V. (1999) Writing as academic literacies: understanding textual practices in higher education, in C.N. Candlin and K. Hyland (eds) *Writing: Texts, Processes and Practices.* London: Longman, pp. 62–81.

LeCourt, D. (1998) Critical pedagogy in the computer classroom: politicizing the writing space, *Computers and Composition*, 15, 275–95.

Leont'ev, A.N. (1981) The problem of activity in psychgology, in J.V. Wertsch (ed.) *The Concept of Activity in Soviet Psychology*. Armonk, NY: M.E. Sharpe, pp. 40–71.

Lillis, T. (1997) New voices in academia? The regulative nature of academic writing conventions, *Language and Education*, 11(3), 182–99.

Lillis, T. (2001) *Student Writing: Access, Regulation, Desire*. London and New York: Routledge.

Lillis, T. and Turner, J. (2001) Student writing in higher education: contemporary confusion, traditional concerns, *Teaching in Higher Education*, 6(1), 57–68.

Marton, F., Hounsell, D. and Entwistle, N. (eds) (1984) *The Experience of Learning*. Edinburgh: Scottish Academic Press.

Mason, R. and Kaye, A. (1989) *Mindweave: Communication, Computers and Distance Education*. Oxford: Pergamon.

Matthews, J. (2005) Visual culture and critical pedagogy in 'terrorist times', *Discourse: Studies in the Cultural Politics of Education*, 26(2), 203–24.

McAndrew, P. (2006) OCI research and evaluation plan. http://kn.open.ac.uk/pub lic/getfile.cfm?documentfileid=10027 (accessed March 2007).

McKenna, C. (2003) From skills to subjects: the reconceptualization of writing development in higher education, in C. Rust (ed.) *Improving Student Learning: Theory and Practice*. Oxford: Oxford Centre for Staff and Learning Development, pp. 67–74.

McKenna, C. (2006) Disrupting the narrative: the hypertext essay as a challenge to academic writing. Academic Literacies Annual Symposium, University of Westminster, June.

Mercer, N. (1995) *The Guided Construction of Knowledge: Talk among Teachers and Learners*. Clevedon: Multilingual Matters.

MIT OpenCourseWare (2005) 2004 evaluation findings report. http:// www.core.org.cn/NR/rdonlyres/90C9BC91–7819–48A0–9E9A-D6B2701C1CE5/0/MIT_OCW_2004_Program_Eval.pdf (accessed March 2007).

Mitchell, S. (2006) Thinking writing: news from the Writing in the Disciplines initiative. Thinking Writing Project, Queen Mary, University of London.

Monroe, J. (2002) *Writing and Revising the Disciplines*. Ithica, NY: Cornell University Press.

National Committee of Inquiry into Higher Education Report (1997) *Higher Education in the Learning Society: Report of the National Committee of Inquiry into Higher Education* (Dearing Report). Leeds NCIHE Publications. http://www.ncl.ac.uk/ncihe/ (accessed March 2007).

Naughton, J. (2007) Writers who work for nothing: it's a licence to print money. *The Observer*, 11 March. http://observer.guardian.co.uk/business/story/0,,2031059,00.html (accessed March 2007).

Negroponte, N. (1995) *Being Digital*. New York, NY: Knopf.

New London Group (1996) A pedagogy of multiliteracies: designing social futures, *Harvard Educational Review*, 66(1), 60–92.

Noble, D.F. (2002) Technology and the commodification of higher education, *Monthly Review*, 53(10). http://www.monthlyreview.org/0302noble.htm (accessed March 2007).

Oliver, M. (2005) Metadata vs educational culture: roles, power and standardisation, in R. Land and S. Bayne (eds) *Education in Cyberspace*. London and New York: RoutledgeFalmer, pp. 72–88.

Oliver, M. and Shaw, M. (2003) Asynchronous discussion in support of medical education, *Journal of Asychnronous Learning Networks*, 7(1), 56–67. http://www.aln.org/publications/jaln/v57n51/pdf/v57n51_oliver.pdf (accessed March 2007).

Oliver, M., Roberts, G., Beetham, H., Ingraham, B., Dyke, M. and Levy, P. (2007) Knowledge, society and perspectives on learning technology, in G. Conole and M. Oliver (eds) *Contemporary Perspectives in E-learning Research: Themes, Methods and Impact on Practice*. London: Routledge, pp. 21–37.

Ong, W. (1982) *Literacy and Orality: The Technologising of the Word*. London & New York: Methuen.

O'Reilly, T. (2005) What is Web 2.0? Design patterns and business models for the next generation of software. http://www.oreillynet.com/pub/a/oreilly/tim/news/2005/09/30/what-is-web-20.html (accessed March 2007).

Pahl, K. and Rowsell, J. (eds) (2006) *Travel Notes from the New Literacy Studies: Case Studies in Practice*. Clevedon: Multilingual Matters.

Paloff, R.M. and Pratt, K. (1999) *Building Learning Communities in Cyberspace*. San Francisco, CA: Jossey-Bass.

Papert, S. (1980) *Mindstorms*. New York, NY: Basic Books.

Pardoe, S. (2000) A question of attribution: the indeterminacy of 'learning from experience', in M.R. Lea and B. Stierer (eds) *Student Writing in Higher Education: New Contexts*. Buckingham: Society for Research into Higher Education/Open University Press, pp. 125–46.

Piaget, J. (1972) *The Psychology of the Child*. New York, NY: Basic Books.

Prensky, M. (2001) Digital natives, Digital Immigrants, *On the Horizon*, 9(5). http://www.marcprensky.com/writing/Prensky%20-%20Digital%20Natives,%20Digital%20Immigrants%20-%20Part1.pdf (accessed January 2007).

Quality Assurance Agency for Higher Education (2001a) Learning from subject review 1993–2001. http://www.qaa.ac.uk/reviews/subjectReview/learningfromSubjectReview/subjectreviewsection2.asp (accessed March 2007).

Quality Assurance Agency for Higher Education (2001b) *Guidelines for HE Progress Files*. http://www.qaa.ac.uk/crntwork/progfileHE/guidelines/progfile2001.pdf (accessed March 2007).

Rai, L. (2006) Owning (up) to reflective writing in social work education, *Social Work Education*, 25(8), 785–97.

Ravenscroft, A. (2005) Towards highly communicative e-learning communities: developing a socio-cultural framework for cognitive change, in R. Land and S. Bayne (eds) *Education in Cyberspace*. London and New York: RoutledgeFalmer, pp. 130–45.

Renninger, K.A. and Shumar, W. (eds) (2002) *Building Virtual Communities: Learning and Change in Cyberspace*. Cambridge: Cambridge University Press.

Rheingold, H. (1993) *The Virtual Community: Homesteading on the Electronic Frontier*. New York, NY: Addison-Wesley. http://www.rheingold.com/vc/book (accessed March 2007).

Rovai, A. (2002) Building sense of community at a distance, *International Review of Research in Open and Distance Learning*, 3(1). http://www.irrodl.org/index.php/irrodl/article/view/79/153 (accessed March 2007).

Rushkoff, D. (1994) *Media Virus: Hidden Agendas in Popular Culture*. New York, NY: Ballantine.

Russell, D. (2002) Looking beyond the interface: activity theory and distributed learning, in: M.R. Lea and K. Nicoll (eds) *Distributed Learning. Social and*

Cultural Approaches to Practice. London and New York: RoutledgeFalmer, pp. 64–82.

Russell, D. (2005) Multimedia online cases: role playing in multiple perspectives across multiple courses. http://mycase.engl.iastate.edu/presentations/Russell4C05.doc (accessed December 2006).

Salganik, M.J., Dodds, P.S. and Watts, D.J. (2006) Experimental study of inequality and unpredictability in an artificial cultural market, *Science*, 311(5762) 854–6. http://www.sciencemag.org/cgi/content/short/311/5762/854 (accessed March 2007).

Salmon, G. (2000) *E-Moderating: The Key to Teaching and Learning Online*. London: Kogan Page.

Schön, D.A. (1983) *The Reflective Practitioner. How Professionals Think in Action*. London: Temple Smith.

Schön, D.A. (1991) *The Reflective Turn: Case Studies in and on Educational Practice*. New York, NY: Teachers College Press.

Scribner, S. and Cole, M. (1981) *The Psychology of Literacy*. Cambridge: MA: Harvard University Press.

Selfe, C.L. (1999) *Technology and Literacy in the Twenty-First Century: The Importance of Paying Attention*. Carbondale, IL: Southern Illinois University Press.

Selfe, C.L. and Hilligoss, S. (eds) (1994) *Literacy and Computers. The Complications of Teaching and Learning with Technology*. New York, NY: Modern Language Association of America.

Sfard, A. (1998) On two metaphors for learning and the dangers of choosing just one, *Educational Researcher*, 27(2), 4–13.

Shaughnessy, M.P. (1977) *Errors and Expectations: A Guide for the Teacher of Basic Writing*. New York. NY: Oxford University Press.

Shiels, M. (1975) Why Johnny can't write, *Newsweek*, 8 December: pp. 58–65.

Smith, M. and Kollock, P. (eds) (1999) *Communities in Cyberspace*. New York, NY: Routledge.

Snyder, I. (2001) A new communication order: researching literary practices in the network society, *Language and Education*, 15(2–3), 117–31.

Snyder, I. (ed.) (2002) *Silicon Literacies: Communication, Innovation and Education in the Electronic Age*. London: Routledge.

Stefani, L. (2005) PDP / CPD and e-portfolios: rising to the challenge of modelling good practice. http://www.alt.ac.uk/docs/lorraine_stefani_paper.doc (accessed March 2007).

Stierer, B. (2000) Schoolteachers as students: academic literacy and the construction of professional knowledge within master's courses in education, in M.R. Lea and B. Stierer (eds) *Student Writing in Higher Education: New Contexts*. Buckingham: Society for Research into Higher Education/Open University Press, pp. 179–95.

Street, B.V. (1984) *Literacy in Theory and Practice*. Cambridge: Cambridge University Press.

Street, B.V. (1995) *Social Literacies: Critical Approaches to Literacy Development, Ethnography and Education*. London: Longman.

Street, B.V. (1996) Multiple literacies and multiliteracies. Keynote address to Domains of Literacy Conference, Institute of Education, London.

Street, B.V. (2003) What's 'new' in New Literacy Studies? Critical approaches to literacy in theory and practice, *Current Issues in Comparative Education*, 5(2).

http://www.tc.columbia.edu/cice/archives/5.2/52street.pdf (accessed March 2007).

Street, B.V. (ed.) (2005) *Literacies across Educational Contexts: Mediating Learning and Teaching.* Philadelphia: Caslon.

Strivens, J. (2005) Efficient assessment of portfolios. Report for Practice-Based Professional Learning Centre for Excellence in Teaching and Learning. *http:// www.open.ac.uk/cetl-workspace/cetlcontent/documents/460d167687b15.pdf* (accessed May 2007).

Sugar, W. and Bonk, C. (1997) Student role play in the World Forum: analyses of an Arctic adventure learning apprenticeship, in C. Bonk and K. King (eds) *Electronic Collaborators: Learner Centered Technologies for Literacy.* Mahwah, NJ: Lawrence Erlbaum Associates, pp 131–56.

Thesen, L. (1994) Voices in discourse: rethinking shared meaning in academic writing. Unpublished MPhil dissertation, University of Cape Town.

Thorpe, M. (2002) From independent learning to collaborative learning: new communities of practice in open, distance and distributed learning, in M.R. Lea and K. Nicoll (eds) *Distributed Learning: Social and Cultural Approaches to Practice.* London and New York: Routledge, pp. 131–51.

Tosh, D., Light, T.P., Fleming, K. and Haywood, J. (2005) Engagement with electronic portfolios: challenges from the student perspective, *Canadian Journal of Learning and Technology,* 31(3). http://www.cjlt.ca/content/vol31.3/tosh.html (accessed March 2007).

Tunbridge, N. (1995) The cyberspace cowboy, *Australian Personal Computer,* 2–4 December.

Turing, A. (1950) Computing machinery and intelligence, *Mind,* 49, 433–60.

UK Grad Programme (2001) Joint statement of the UK research councils training requirements for research students. http://www.grad.ac.uk/downloads/documents/general/Joint%20Skills%20Statement.pdf (accessed March 2007).

Usher, R. (2000) Flexible learning, postmodernity and the contemporary workplace, in V. Jakupec and J. Garrick (eds) *Flexible Learning, Human Resource and Organisational Development: Putting Theory to Work.* London: Routledge. pp. 225–38.

Vygotsky, L. (1978) *Mind in Society.* Cambridge, MA: Harvard University Press.

Wallace, R. (2003) Online learning in higher education – a review of research on interactions among teachers and students, *Education, Communication and Information,* 3(2), 241–80.

Walton, M. (2004) Behind the screen: the language of web design, in I. Snyder and C. Beavis (eds) *Doing Literacy Online: Teaching, Learning and Playing in an Electronic World.* Cresskill, NJ: Hampton Press, pp. 91–120.

Walton, M. and Archer, A. (2004) The Web and information literacy: scaffolding the use of web sources in a project-based curriculum, *British Journal of Educational Technology,* 35(2), 173–86.

Wegerif, R. and Scrimshaw, P. (1997) *Computers and Talk in the Primary Classroom.* Clevedon: Multilingual Matters.

Weller, M. (2007) *Virtual Learning Environments – Using, Choosing and Developing your VLE.* London: Routledge.

Weller, M., Pegler, C. and Mason, R. (2003) Working with learning objects: some pedagogical suggestions. Communications of Practice ALT-C, University of Sheffield and Sheffield Hallam University.

Wellman, B. and Gulia, M. (1999) Virtual communities as communities: net surfers don't ride alone, in M.S.P. Kollock (ed.) *Communities in Cyberspace.* New York, NY: Routledge, pp. 167–94.

Wenger, E. (1987) *Artificial Intelligence and Tutoring Systems.* Los Altos, CA: Morgan Kaufmann.

Wenger, E. (1998) *Communities of Practice* Cambridge: Cambridge University Press.

Wiley, D. (2002) The coming collision between automated instruction and social constructivism. http://telr-research.osu.edu/learning_objects/documents/Wiley.pdf (accessed March 2007).

Winograd, T. and Flores, F. (1986) *Understanding Computers and Cognition* Norwood, NJ: Ablex.

Young, M., Barab, S. and Garrett, S. (2000) Agent as detector: an ecological psychology perspective on learning by perceiving-acting systems, in D. Jonassen and S. Land (eds) *Theoretical Foundations of Learning Environments.* Mahwah, NJ: Lawrence Erlbaum Associates, pp. 147–72.

Zemsky, R. and Massy, W. (2004) Thwarted innovation: what happened to e-learning and why. Weatherstation Project, University of Pennsylvania. http://www.irhe.upenn.edu/Docs/Jun2004/ThwartedInnovation.pdf. (accessed May 2007).

Author index

Subject index

The Society for Research into Higher Education

The Society for Research into Higher Education (SRHE), an international body, exists to stimulate and co-ordinate research into all aspects of higher education. It aims to improve the quality of higher education through the encouragement of debate and publication on issues of policy, on the organization and management of higher education institutions, and on the curriculum, teaching and learning methods.

The Society is entirely independent and receives no subsidies, although individual events often receive sponsorship from business or industry. The Society is financed through corporate and individual subscriptions and has members from many parts of the world. It is an NGO of UNESCO.

Under the imprint *SRHE & Open University Press*, the Society is a specialist publisher of research, having over 80 titles in print. In addition to *SRHE News*, the Society's newsletter, the Society publishes three journals: *Studies in Higher Education* (three issues a year), *Higher Education Quarterly* and *Research into Higher Education Abstracts* (three issues a year).

The Society runs frequent conferences, consultations, seminars and other events. The annual conference in December is organized, at and, with a higher education institution. There are a growing number of networks which focus on particular areas of interest, including:

Access	FE/HE
Assessment	Graduate Employment
Consultants	New Technology for Learning
Curriculum Development	Postgraduate Issues
Eastern European	Quantitative Studies
Educational Development Research	Student Development

Benefits to members

Individual

- The opportunity to participate in the Society's networks
- Reduced rates for the annual conferences
- Free copies of *Research into Higher Education Abstracts*
- Reduced rates for *Studies in Higher Education*

- Reduced rates for *Higher Education Quarterly*
- Free online access to *Register of Members' Research Interests* – includes valuable reference material on research being pursued by the Society's members
- Free copy of occasional in-house publications, e.g. *The Thirtieth Anniversary Seminars Presented by the Vice-Presidents*
- Free copies of *SRHE News* and *International News* which inform members of the Society's activities and provides a calendar of events, with additional material provided in regular mailings
- A 35 per cent discount on all SRHE/Open University Press books
- The opportunity for you to apply for the annual research grants
- Inclusion of your research in the *Register of Members' Research Interests*

Corporate

- Reduced rates for the annual conference
- The opportunity for members of the Institution to attend SRHE's network events at reduced rates
- Free copies of *Research into Higher Education Abstracts*
- Free copies of *Studies in Higher Education*
- Free online access to *Register of Members' Research Interests* – includes valuable reference material on research being pursued by the Society's members
- Free copy of occasional in-house publications
- Free copies of *SRHE News* and *International News*
- A 35 per cent discount on all SRHE/Open University Press books
- The opportunity for members of the Institution to submit applications for the Society's research grants
- The opportunity to work with the Society and co-host conferences
- The opportunity to include in the *Register of Members' Research Interests* your Institution's research into aspects of higher education

Membership details: SRHE, 76 Portland Place, London W1B 1NT, UK Tel: 020 7637 2766. Fax: 020 7637 2781. email: srheoffice@srhe.ac.uk
World Wide Web: http://www.srhe.ac.uk./srhe/
Catalogue: SRHE & Open University Press, McGraw-Hill Education, McGraw-Hill House, Shoppenhangers Road, Maidenhead, Berkshire SL6 2QL. Tel: 01628 502500. Fax: 01628 770224. email: enquiries@openup.co.uk – web: www.openup.co.uk